3.95

SAYYID ABUL A' LA MAWDUDI

**Books are to be returned on or before
the last date below.**

LIBREX —

The Islamic J

D1331655

Published by
The Islamic Foundation
Markfield Conference Centre
Ratby Lane, Markfield
Leicester LE67 9SY, United Kingdom
Tel: 01530 244944/5   Fax: 01530-244946
E-mail: i.foundation@islamic-foundation.org.uk
Publication E-mail: publications@islamic-foundation.com
Website: http://www.islamic-foundation.org.uk/

Quran House, P.O.Box 30611, Nairobi, Kenya
P.M.B. 3193, Kano, Nigeria

The Islamic way of life (new English version) 1986
Revised and extended English translation of
Urdu *Islām kā Niẓām Ḥayāt* (Lahore, 1967).
Reprinted 1992, 2001

Edited and translated: Khurshid Ahmad and Khurram Murad

© The Islamic Foundation

British Library cataloguing in Publication Data
Mawdudi, Sayyid Abul A'la
The Islamic way of life
1. Religious life (Islam)
I. Title II Ahmad, Khurshid II. Murad, Khurram IV. Islām kā
Ḥayāt English
297'.44BP188

ISBN 0 86037 177-8 (PB)
ISBN 0 86037 176-X (HB)

Cover Design: Nasir Cadir

Contents

Foreword

During January–March, 1948, Sayyid Abul A'la Maw-dudi (1903–1979) gave a series of five talks, in Urdu, on Radio Pakistan, in which he dealt with the broad and basic principles of the moral, political, economic, social and spiritual teachings of Islam. They were immediately published in book form under the title *Islām kā Niẓām Ḥayāt* (Lahore, 1948), and have since been reprinted many times, both separately and as a part of a larger collection of Sayyid Mawdudi's works, *Islām kā Niẓām Zindigī* (Lahore, 1962).

These talks have also been translated into several different languages, the first English translation appearing in 1950. A greatly improved version was produced by the Islamic Research Academy, Karachi under the title *The Islamic Way of Life* (Lahore, 1967). It contained a new translation and an additional chapter on the Islamic Concept of Life, compiled from various writings of Sayyid Mawdudi and providing a concise introduction to the view of man and universe as given in the Divine guidance, which forms the basis of the Islamic way of life. This additional material (contributed by Khurshid Ahmad) was intended to guide the reader to a clearer and better understanding of the basis and content of Sayyid Mawdudi's short radio talks.

Now an entirely new and more extended English edition is being published by the Islamic Foundation. If differs from the earlier edition in two main respects. Firstly, although the language of the earlier translation was quite satisfactory, we have taken this opportunity to improve it further. We believe that it now reads much better. More importantly, extensive references from the Qur'ān and Hadith have been provided (by Khurram Murad) to some of the important ideas expounded by Sayyid Mawdudi. This, *inshā' Allah*, will greatly add to the value and usefulness of the original.

The Islamic Way of Life is an immensely important book. It has been widely acclaimed and used as one of the best and most concise primary introductory texts on Islam in contemporary times. Within the limits of five very short radio talks, Sayyid Mawdudi has said, succinctly and effectively, what others might have needed volumes to express. He has brought together most of the essential, salient teachings of Islam on the major human responsibilities. Whether it be morals and ethics, politics and economics, family and social life, or spirituality and worship, the reader will find here a comprehensive and coherent introduction to underlying principles as well as the broad outlines of how these are to be translated into concrete terms. Perhaps it may not be an exaggeration to say that no other work, in any language, deals with so wide a range of themes in so short a space as does this work of Sayyid Mawdudi.

Sayyid Mawdudi was blessed not only with erudition and scholarship but with brilliant gifts of exposition. Hence, despite the enormous agenda he set for himself, this brief work nevertheless exhibits all the passionate lucidity and the persuasive logic so characteristic of his style. That style has its own charm, yet the argument it carries remains deeply convincing and compelling in its appeal. Such a discourse does not take long to penetrate and capture hearts and minds. Its impact has not been limited to merely intellectual persuasion, nor was it the author's intention that it should. It has inspired many to commit themselves to their Creator and strive to shape their total lives by His guidance. They have all found it extremely useful to educate and enrich themselves, and have widely used it as such.

Obviously what such a short work could not include are references to the original sources of the Qur'ān and Hadith from which Sayyid Mawdudi derived all that he has propounded. This task he accomplished fully and most ably, in the longer pieces that he wrote, throughout his life, on these very topics, and to which the reader will find ample references within the text. Special mention must be made in this respect of his monumental eight-volume commentary on the Qur'ān in Urdu, the *Tafhīmul Qur'ān* (Lahore, 1949–1972). There one can find ample and convincing evidence that whatever Sayyid Mawdudi has said is based on the Qur'ān and Hadith.

Unfortunately most of this material is not yet available to the ordinary English reader who needs, nevertheless, to see for himself how Sayyid Mawdudi argues his position from the basic texts of Islam. This aim might have been served better perhaps by translating the relevant extracts from the other writings and including them here. But this would have been a long, ambitious project. We hope that one day, *insha' Allah*, all of his writings will be available in English. For the present, we felt it would be more feasible, and also more immediately useful, to provide direct references from the Qur'ān. Hence the extensive notes.

Although there can be little doubt that almost all these notes have been derived from, and certainly inspired by, Sayyid Mawdudi's own writings, it is only fair to say that he bears no responsibility whatever for any error or blemish in them. The editor (Khurram Murad) who has provided them alone remains responsible for everything included therein.

We expect that this work will continue to be used, as it has been so far, by the generations of Muslims who are ardently striving to make their lives and social orders truly Islamic. In many groups, study circles, classes and organisations around the world it will be eagerly taken up as a basic text. We consider it most essential, however, that all studies on Islam are pursued, as far as possible, within the framework of the Qur'ān and Hadith. Only these should remain as the absolute and normative sources for guidance and reference. To these the Muslim youth, intelligentsia and scholars must turn again and again and draw closer and closer. It is our earnest prayer that these notes may provide the necessary framework, and encourage the readers into a more direct and intimate relationship with the word of God.

This edition is being produced at a time when the Islamic social order has become a crucial issue on a global scale. On one side, Muslims almost everywhere are in an anxious struggle to shape their lives by the guidance given by the Creator through His Messengers. It would be naive to brush aside the huge and complex problems that Muslims face in this regard in view of the tremendous changes wrought in human life by technological advances and the climate created by Western domination, whose character is an arrogant secularism in rebellion against God expressed in slogans like 'man has come of age'. Are Muslims out of step with the times if they still turn to God for guidance in the conduct of their personal and social affairs? What do the Qur'ān and Hadith have to offer? Although there can be no mistaking the signs as to which way the tide is flowing, a clear and firm course has yet to be charted by the Muslim societies towards the actualisation of Islam in their lives. The various attempts so far made cannot be taken to finally define the ultimate pattern that may finally emerge. But Sayyid Mawdudi's present work must remain an important, pioneering effort, whose importance will never diminish.

On the other side, the 'West' (by which we do not mean simply a geographical territory but a world-view, a faith, and a culture), though still very much in power, has demonstrated its utter barrenness in producing a social order that will ensure peace and happiness for humanity. Indeed, it has put the very survival of humanity in doubt. The divorce between God and public life, between Divine guidance and human knowledge, has given rise to social relations and technologies that have brought man to the precipice of self-annihilation. This is the more tragic because as far as the 'individual' is concerned, Western civilisation turned him long ago into a prey of anxiety, dread and alienation. Furthermore, the West continues to live, unfortunately, and quite unnecessarily, in self-inflicted dread of the Muslims' effort to shape their destiny in accordance with Islam.

We hope that, at this juncture, this book will enable Muslim and Western readers alike to develop a grasp of the ideals, principles and values which shape Islamic culture and society, clear up some misunderstandings and fears, and point to some fruitful pathways for the future of mankind.

We record our thanks to all those friends and critics who have helped us in revising this book, from its very early stages in the 1960s, in particular to Muhammad Zubair, Umer Chapra, Ashraf Abu Turab, P. Phillips and Paul Moorman.

We pray to Allah *subhanahu wata'ala* to bless our effort with His forgiveness and mercy.

Leicester
20 May, 1986
11 Ramadan al-Mubarak, 1406

Khurshid Ahmad

Khurram Murad

1

The Islamic Concept of Life

The chief characteristic of Islam is that it makes no distinction between the spiritual and the secular in life. Its aim is to shape both individual lives as well as society as a whole in ways that will ensure that the Kingdom of God may really be established on earth and that peace, contentment and wellbeing may fill the world. The Islamic way of life is thus based on a unique concept of man's place in the universe. That is why it is necessary that, before we discuss the moral, social, political and economic systems of Islam, we should have a clear idea of what that concept is.

1

BASIC PRINCIPLES

1   God, who is the Creator, the Ruler and the Lord of the universe, has created man and provided him with a temporary home in that part of His vast kingdom which is the earth. He has endowed man with the faculties of thinking and understanding, and has given him the power to distinguish right from wrong. Man has also been invested with free will and the power to use the resources of the world however he likes. That is, man has a measure of autonomy, while being at the same time God's representative on earth.

This chapter has been compiled in its present form by selections from the writings of Sayyid Abul A'lā Mawdudī by Khurshid Ahmad.

2   Before assigning to man this vicegerency (*Khilāfat*), God made it clear to him that He alone was the Lord, the Ruler and the Deity. As such, the entire universe and all the creatures in it (including man) should submit to Him alone. Man must not think himself totally free and must realise that this earth is not his permanent abode. He has been created to live on it only for a probationary period and, in due course, he will return to his Lord, to be judged according to the way he has spent that period. The only right course for man is to acknowledge God as the only Lord, the Sustainer and the Deity, and to follow His guidance and His commands in all he does. His sole objective should be to merit the approval of Allah.

If man follows a course of righteousness and godliness (which he is *free* to choose and follow) he will be rewarded in this world and the next: in this world he will live a life of peace and contentment, and in the Hereafter he will qualify for the heaven of eternal bliss, *al-Jannah*. If he chooses to follow the course of godlessness and evil (which he is equally *free* to choose and follow), his life will be one of corruption and frustration in this world, and in the life to come he will face the prospect of that abode of pain and misery which is called Hell.

3   After making this position clear, God set man on earth and provided the very first human beings (Adam[1] and Eve) with guidance as to how they were to live. Thus man's life on this earth did not start in utter darkness. From the beginning a bright torch of light was provided so that humanity could fulfil its glorious destiny. The very first man received revealed knowledge from God Himself, and was told the correct way to live. This code of life was Islam, the attitude of complete submission to Allah, the Creator of man and the whole universe. It was this religion which Adam, the first man, passed down to posterity.

But later generations gradually drifted away from the right path. Either they lost the original teachings through negligence or they deliberately adulterated and distorted them. They associated God with innumerable human beings, material objects and imaginary gods. *Shirk* (polytheism) became widespread. They mixed up the teachings of God with myths and strange philosophies and thus produced a jumble of religions and cults; and they discarded the God-given principles of personal and social morality, the Shari'ah.

4   Although man departed from the path of truth, disregarded or distorted the Shari'ah or even rejected the code of Divine guidance, God did not destroy them or *force* them to take the right course. Forced morality was not in keeping with the autonomy He had given to man. Instead, God *appointed* certain good people from among the human society itself to guide men to the right path. These men believed in God, and lived a life of obedience to Him. He honoured them by His revelations, giving them the knowledge of reality. Known as prophets, blessings and peace be on all of them, they were assigned the task of spreading God's message among men.

5   Many thousands of these prophets were raised throughout the ages, in all lands and in all nations. All of them brought the same message, all of them advocated the same way of life, (*dīn*), that is, the way which was revealed to man on the first day of his existence. All of them had the same mission: they called men to Islam – to submit to God alone, asked those who accepted the Divine guidance to live in accordance with it and organised them into a movement for the establishment of the Divine law, and for putting an end to all deviations from the true path. Many people, however, refused to accept their guidance and many of those who did accept it gradually drifted away from their initial commitment.

6   Lastly, God raised the Prophet Muhammad, blessings and peace be on him, in Arabia to complete the mission of the earlier prophets. The message of Muhammad, blessings and peace be on him, was for the whole of mankind. He presented anew the teachings of Islam in their pristine form and provided humanity once again with the Divine guidance which had been largely lost. He organised all those who accepted his message into one community (Ummah), charged with living in accordance with the teachings of Islam, with calling humanity to the path of righteousness and with establishing the supremacy of the word of God on earth. This guidance is enshrined in the Holy Qur'ān.[2]

11

Iman: Its Nature and Character

The Qur'ān deals in many passages with man's relationship to Allah and the concept of life which naturally follows from that relationship. Its message is epitomised in the following verse:

> Verily Allah hath bought of the Believers their lives and their properties for the price that theirs shall be the Paradise: so they fight in the way of Allah and slay and are slain. It (i.e. the promise of Paradise) is a covenant which is binding on Him in the Torāh and the Injīl and the Qur'ān. And who is more faithful unto his covenant than Allah? Rejoice then in your bargain that ye have made, for that is the supreme triumph. (al-Tawbah 9: 111)

In the above verse the nature of the relationship which comes into existence between man and God because of Iman (the belief, trust and faith in Allah) is called a 'bargain'. This means that Iman in Allah is not a mere metaphysical concept; it is in the nature of a *contract* by which man barters his life and his possessions in exchange for the promise of Paradise in the Hereafter. God, as it were, purchases a Believer's life and property and promises, in return, the reward of Paradise in the life after death. This concept of a bargain and a covenant has important implications, and needs to be clearly understood.

Everything in this world belongs to Allah. As such, man's life and wealth, which are part of this world, also belong to Him, because He has created them and has entrusted them to every man for his use. Looked at from this angle, the question of 'selling' or 'buying' may not seem to arise at all; God does not need to buy what is already His and man cannot sell what is not really his.

But there is one thing which *has* been conferred on man, and which *now* belongs fully to him, and that is *free will*, which gives him freedom to choose between following or not following the path of Allah. This freedom of will and choice does not automatically make man the real owner of all the power and resources over which he has command, nor does it give him the right to use them just as he likes. Yet, because of this free will, he may, if he likes, consider himself free of all obligations to the Lord and independent of any higher authority. It is here that the question of *bargain* arises.

This bargain thus does not mean that God is purchasing something which belongs to man. Its real nature is this: all creation belongs to God but He has bestowed certain things on man to be used by him on trust. God wants man to willingly and voluntarily acknowledge this. A person who voluntarily renounces his freedom to reject God's supremacy and instead acknowledges His sovereignty, and, in so doing, 'sells' his 'autonomy' (which, too, is a gift from God) to God, will get in return God's promise of eternal bliss in Paradise. A person who makes such a bargain is a Mu'min (Believer) and Iman (faith) is the Islamic name for this contract; a person who chooses not to enter into this contract, or who, after making such a contract, does not keep to it, is a Kafir. The avoidance or abrogation of the contract is technically known as Kufr.

Such is the nature of the contract. Now let us briefly study its various aspects and stipulations.

1   God has set us to account for ourselves in two areas:

(*a*)   He has left man free, but nonetheless wishes to see whether he will remain honest and loyal to Him, or whether he will rebel against his own Creator, whether he will behave nobly or start 'playing such fantastic tricks as make the angels weep'.[3]

(*b*)   He wants to see whether man is prepared to have enough trust in God to offer his life and wealth in return for a promise about the next world.

2   It is a principle of Islamic law that Iman consists in adherence to a certain set of doctrines and anyone who accepts those doctrines becomes a Mu'min. No one has the right to call such a man a disbeliever or drive him from the fold of Ummah, unless there is clear proof that faith has been abandoned. This is the legal position. But in the eyes of the

13

Lord, Iman is only valid when it entails complete surrender of one's will and freedom of choice to the will of Allah. It is a state of thought and action, coming from the heart, wherein man submits himself fully to Allah, renouncing all claim to his own supremacy.

A man may recite the *Kalimah*,[4] accept the contract and even offer Prayers and perform other acts of worship, but if in his heart he regards himself as the owner and the master of his physical and mental powers and of his moral and material resources, then, however much the people may look upon him as a Mu'min, in the eyes of God he will be a disbeliever. He will not really have entered into the bargain which the Qur'ān says is the essence of Iman. If a man does not use his powers and resources in the way God has prescribed for him, using them instead in pursuits which God has forbidden, it is clear that either he has not pledged his life and property to Allah, or has nullified that pledge by his conduct.

3   This aspect of Iman makes the Islamic way of life the very *opposite of* that of the non-Muslim. A Muslim, who has real faith in Allah, makes his entire life one of obedience and surrender to His will. He never behaves arrogantly or selfishly or as if he were master of his own destiny, save in moments of forgetfulness. And as soon as he becomes conscious of such a lapse, he will submit himself to his Lord and ask forgiveness for his error.

Similarly, a group of people or a society which consists of true Muslims can never break away from the Law of their Lord. Its political order, its social organisations, its culture, its economic policy, its legal system and its international strategy must all be in tune with the code of guidance revealed by Allah. Any unwitting contraventions must be corrected as soon as they are realised.

It is disbelievers who feel free from God's guidance and behave as if they were their own master. Anyone who behaves like this, even though he may bear a name similar to that of a Muslim, is treading the path of the disbelievers.

4   The will of God, which it is obligatory for man to follow, is the one which God Himself has revealed for man's guidance. It cannot be determined by man himself. God has

Himself explained it clearly and there is no ambiguity about it. Therefore, if a society sticks honestly to its contract with Allah, it must shape its life in accordance with the Book of God and the Sunnah of the Prophet, blessings and peace be on him.

It is clear from the foregoing discussion why the payment of the 'price' has been postponed till the life after death. Paradise is not the reward for the *mere profession* of the bargain, it is the reward for the faithful *execution* of it. Unless the behaviour of the 'vendor' complies with the terms of the contract he will not be entitled to the reward. The final act of the 'sale' can only be concluded after the last moment of the vendor's earthly life.

There is another significant point which emerges from the study of the verse quoted above when it is read in its context in the Qur'ān. In the verses preceding it, reference is made to the people who professed Iman and promised a life of obedience, but who, when the hour of trial came, proved unequal to the task. Some neglected the call of the hour and betrayed the cause. Others refused to sacrifice their lives and riches in the cause of Allah. The Qur'ān, after criticising their insincerity, makes it clear that Iman is a contract, a form of pledge between man and God. It does not consist in a mere profession of belief in Allah. It is an acknowledgement of the fact that Allah alone is our Lord, Sovereign and Ruler and that everything that man has, including his own life, belongs to Him and must be used in accordance with His directives. If a Muslim adopts a different course, he is insincere in his profession of faith. Only those who have *really* sold their lives and all that they possess to God and who follow His dictates in all spheres of activity can be called true Believers.[5]

3

THE SCHEME OF LIFE

In Islam, man's entire individual and social life is an exercise in developing and strengthening his relationship with

God. Iman, the starting point of our religion, consists in the acceptance of this relationship by man's intellect and will; Islam means submission to the will of God in all aspects of life. The Islamic code of conduct is known as the Shari'ah. Its sources are the Qur'ān and the Sunnah of the Prophet, blessings and peace be on him.[6]

The final Book of God and His final Messenger stand today as the repositories of this truth. Everyone who agrees that the concept of Reality stated by the Prophet, and the Holy Book is true, should step forward and surrender himself to the will of God. It is this submission which is called *Islām*, the result of Iman in actual life. And those who of their own free will accept God as their Sovereign, surrender to His Divine will and undertake to regulate their lives in accordance with His commandments, are called *Muslims*.

All those persons who thus surrender themselves are welded into a community and that is how the 'Muslim society' comes into being. It is an ideological society, radically different from those which are founded on the basis of race, colour or territory. It is the result of a deliberate choice, the outcome of a 'contract' which takes place between human beings and their Creator. Those who enter into this contract undertake to recognise God as their Sovereign, His guidance as supreme and His injunctions as absolute Law. They also undertake to accept, without question, His word as to what is good or evil, right or wrong, permissible or prohibited. In short, freedoms of the Islamic society are limited by the commandments of the Omniscient God. In other words, it is God and not man whose will is the primary source of Law in a Muslim society.

When such a society comes into existence, the Book and the Messenger prescribe for it a code of life called the Shari'ah, and this society is bound to conform to it by virtue of the contract it has entered into. It is, therefore, inconceivable that a real Muslim society can deliberately adopt any other system of life than that based on the Shari'ah. If it does so, its contract is *ipso facto* broken and it becomes 'un-Islamic'.

But we must clearly distinguish between the everyday sins of the individual and a deliberate revolt against the Shari'ah. The former may not mean a breaking up of the contract, while the latter most certainly would. The point that should be clearly understood is that if an Islamic society consciously resolves not to accept the Shari'ah, and decides to enact its own constitution and laws or borrows them from any other source in disregard of the Shari'ah, such a society breaks its contract with God and forfeits its right to be called 'Islamic'.

4

OBJECTIVES AND CHARACTERISTICS

The main objectives of the Shari'ah are to ensure that human life is based on *ma'rūfāt* (good) and to cleanse it of *munkarāt* (evils). The term *ma'rūfāt* denotes all the qualities that have always been accepted as 'good' by the human conscience. Conversely, the word *munkarāt* denotes all those qualities that have always been condemned by human nature as 'evil'. In short, the *ma'rūfāt* are in harmony with human nature and the *munkarāt* are against nature. The Shari'ah gives precise definitions of *ma'rūfāt* and *munkarāt*, clearly indicating the standards of goodness to which individuals and society should aspire.

It does not, however, limit itself to an inventory of good and evil deeds; rather, it lays down an entire scheme of life whose aim is to make sure that good flourishes and evils do not destroy or harm human life.

To achieve this, the Shari'ah has embraced in its scheme everything that encourages the growth of good and has recommended ways to remove obstacles that might prevent this growth. This process gives rise to a subsidiary series of *ma'rūfāt* consisting of ways of initiating and nurturing the good, and yet another set of *ma'rūfāt* consisting of prohibitions in relation to those things which act as impediments to good. Similarly, there is a subsidiary list of *munkarāt* which might initiate or allow the growth of evil.

The Shari'ah shapes Islamic society in a way conducive to the unfettered growth of good, righteousness and truth in every sphere of human activity. At the same time it removes

17

all the impediments along the path to goodness. And it attempts to eradicate corruption from its social scheme by prohibiting evil, by removing the causes of its appearance and growth, by closing the inlets through which it creeps into a society and by adopting deterrent measures to check its occurrence.

Ma'rūfāt

The Shari'ah divides *ma'rūfāt* into three categories: the mandatory (*farḍ* and *wājib*), the recommendatory (*mandūb*) and the permissible (*mubāḥ*).

The observance of the mandatory is obligatory on a Muslim society and the Shari'ah has given clear and binding directions about this. The recommendatory *ma'rūfāt* are those which the Shari'ah expects a Muslim society to observe and practise. Some of them have been very clearly demanded of us while others have been recommended by implication and inference from the sayings of the Prophet, blessings and peace be on him. Besides this, special arrangements have been made for the growth and encouragement of some of them in the scheme of life advocated by the Shari'ah. Others again have simply been recommended by the Shari'ah, leaving it to the society or to its more virtuous elements to look to promote them.

This leaves us with the permissible *ma'rūfāt*. Strictly speaking, according to the Shari'ah everything which has not been expressly prohibited is a permissible *ma'rūf*. Consequently, the sphere of permissible *ma'rūfāt* is very wide, so much so that except for the things specifically prohibited by the Shari'ah, everything is permissible for a Muslim. And in this vast sphere we have been given freedom to legislate according to our own discretion to suit the requirements of our age and conditions.

Munkarāt

The *munkarāt* (the things prohibited in Islam) have been grouped into two categories: things which have been prohibited absolutely (*ḥarām*), and things which are simply undesirable (*makrūh*).

18

Muslims have been enjoined by clear and mandatory injunctions to refrain totally from everything that has been declared *harām*. As for the *makrūh*, the Shari'ah signifies its disapproval either expressly or by implication, giving an indication also as to the extent of such disapproval. For example, there are some *makrūh* things bordering on *harām*, while others are closer to acts which are permissible. Moreover, in some cases, explicit measures have been prescribed by the Shari'ah for the prevention of *makrūh* things, while in others such measures have been left to the discretion of the society or individual.

Some Other Characteristics

The Shari'ah thus prescribes directives for the regulation of our individual as well as collective lives. These directives affect such varied subjects as religious rituals, personal character, morals, habits, family relationships, social and economic affairs, administration, the rights and duties of citizens, the judicial system, the laws of war and peace and international relations. They tell us what is good and bad; what is beneficial and useful and what is injurious and harmful; what are the virtues which we have to cultivate and encourage and what are the evils which we have to suppress and guard against; what is the sphere of our voluntary, personal and social action and what are its limits; and, finally, what methods we can adopt to establish a dynamic order of society and what methods we should avoid. The Shari'ah is a complete way of life and an all-embracing social order.

Another remarkable feature of the Shari'ah is that it is an organic whole. The entire way of life propounded by Islam is animated by the same spirit and hence any arbitrary division of the scheme is bound to affect the spirit as well as the structure of the Islamic order. In this respect, it might be compared to the human body. A leg separated from the body cannot be called one-eighth or one-sixth man, because after its separation from the body the leg cannot perform its function. Nor can it be placed in the body of some other animal with the aim of making it human to the extent of that limb. Likewise, we cannot form a correct judgement about the utility, efficiency and beauty of the hand, the eye or the nose of a human being outside the context of their place and function within the living body.

The same can be said about the scheme of life envisaged by the Shari'ah. Islam signifies a complete way of life which cannot be split up into separate parts. Consequently, it is neither appropriate to consider the different parts of the Shari'ah in isolation, nor to take any particular part and bracket it with any other 'ism'. The Shari'ah can function smoothly only if one's whole life is lived in accordance with it.[7]

2

The Moral System of Islam

A moral sense is inborn in man and, through the ages, it has served as the common man's standard of moral behaviour, approving certain qualities and condemning others. While this instinctive faculty may vary from person to person, human conscience[1] has consistently declared certain moral qualities to be good and others to be bad.

Justice, courage and truthfulness have always found praise, and history does not record any period worth the name in which falsehood, injustice, dishonesty and breach of trust have been praised; sympathy, compassion, loyalty and generosity have always been valued, while selfishness, cruelty, meanness and bigotry have never been approved of by society; men have always appreciated perseverance, determination and courage, but never impatience, fickleness, cowardice and stupidity. Dignity, restraint, politeness and friendliness have throughout the ages been counted virtues, whereas snobbery and rudeness have always been looked down upon. People with a sense of responsibility and devotion to duty have always won the highest regard, those who are incompetent, lazy and lacking in a sense of duty have never been looked upon with approval.

Similarly, in assessing the standards of good and bad in the collective behaviour of society as a whole, only those societies have been considered worthy of honour which have possessed the virtues of organisation, discipline, mutual affection and compassion and which have established a social

.   *This is a new and revised translation of a talk given by the author on Radio Pakistan, Lahore, on 6th January, 1948.*

order based on justice, freedom and equality. Disorganisation, indiscipline, anarchy, disunity, injustice and social privilege have always been considered manifestations of decay and disintegration in a society. Robbery, murder, larceny, adultery and corruption have always been condemned. Slander and blackmail have never been considered healthy social activities, while service and care of the aged, helping one's relatives, regard for neighbours, loyalty to friends, aiding the weak, the destitute and the orphans, and nursing the sick are qualities which have been highly valued since the dawn of civilisation.

Individuals who are honest, sincere and dependable, whose deeds match their words, who are content with their own rightful possessions, who are prompt in the discharge of their obligations to others, who live in peace and let others live in peace, and from whom nothing but good can be expected, have always formed the basis of any healthy human society.

These examples show that human moral standards are universal and have been well-known to mankind throughout the ages.[2] Good and evil are not myths, but realities well understood by all. A sense of good and evil is inherent in the very nature of man. Hence in the terminology of the Qur'ān good is called *ma'rūf* (a well-known thing) and evil *munkar* (an unknown thing); that is to say, good is known to be desirable and evil is known not to commend itself in any way. As the Qur'ān says: *God has revealed to human nature the consciousness and cognition of good and evil.* (al-Shams 91: 8)

Why Differences?

The question that now arises is: if what constitutes good and evil is so clear and universally agreed, why do varying patterns of moral behaviour exist in the world? Why are there so many conflicting moral philosophies? Why do certain moral standards contradict each other? What lies at the root of their differences? What is the unique position of Islam in the context of other ethical systems? On what grounds can we claim that Islam has a perfect moral system? And what exactly is the distinctive contribution of Islam in the realm of ethics?

22

Although these are important questions and must be squarely faced, justice cannot be done to them in the brief span of this talk.[3] So I shall restrict myself to a summary of some of the points crucial to any critical examination of contemporary ethical systems and conflicting patterns of moral behaviour:

(*a*) Through their failure to prescribe specific limits and roles for the various moral virtues and values, present-day moral structures cannot provide a balanced and coherent plan of social conduct.

(*b*) The real cause of the differences in the moral systems seems to lie in their offering different standards for judging what constitutes good and bad actions and in their laying down different ways to distinguish good from evil. Differences also exist in respect of the sanction behind the moral law and in regard to the motives which impel a person to follow it.

(*c*) On deeper reflection we find that the grounds for these differences emerge from different peoples' conflicting views and concepts of the universe, the place of man in it, and of man's purpose on earth. The various systems of ethics, philosophy and religion are in fact a record of the vast divergence of views on such vital questions as: Is there a God of the universe and, if there is, is He the only one or are there many gods? What. are the Divine attributes? What is the nature of the relationship between God and human beings? Has He made any arrangements for guiding humanity through the vicissitudes of life or not? Is man answerable to Him or not? And if so, in what spheres of his life? Is there an ultimate aim of man's creation which he should keep in view throughout his life? Answers to these questions will determine the way of life, the ethical philosophy and the pattern of moral behaviour of the individual and society.

It is difficult for me, in this brief talk, to take stock of the various ethical systems in the world and indicate what solutions each one of them has proposed to these questions and what has been the impact of these answers on the moral evolution of the society believing in these concepts. Here I have to confine myself to the Islamic concept only.[4]

The Islamic Concept of Life and Morality

The viewpoint of Islam is that the universe is the creation of God who is One. He alone is its Master, Sovereign and Sustainer, and it is functioning under His command. He is All-powerful and Omniscient, He is *Subbūh* and *Quddūs* (that is, free from all defects, mistakes, weaknesses and faults and is holy in every respect). His godhood is free from partiality and injustice.[5]

Man is His creature, subject and servant and is born to serve and obey Him. The correct course of life for man is to live in complete obedience to Him. And it is for God, not man, to determine the mode of that worship and obedience.[6]

At certain times God has raised Prophets for the guidance of humanity and has revealed His books through them. It is the duty of man to live his life according to the dictates of God and to follow the Divine guidance.[7]

Man is answerable to God for all his actions and will be called on to render an account of them in the Hereafter. Man's short life on earth is really an opportunity to prepare for that great test. He will be impartially assessed on his conduct in life by a Being who keeps a complete record not merely of his movements and actions and their influence on all that is in the world – from the tiniest speck of dust to the highest mountains – but also of his innermost thoughts and feelings and intentions.[8]

The Goal of Moral Effort

This concept of the universe and of man's place in it indicates the real and ultimate good which should be the object of all mankind's endeavours – 'seeking the pleasure of God'. This is the standard by which Islam judges all conduct. It means that man is not left like a ship without moorings at the mercy of winds and tides; instead, we have a set of unchangeable norms for all moral actions. Moreover, by making the 'pleasure of God' the object of man's life, unlimited possibilities are opened for man's moral evolution, untainted by narrow selfishness or racism or chauvinism.[9]

Islam also furnishes us with the means to determine good

24

and evil conduct. It does not base our knowledge of evil and virtue on mere intellect, desire, intuition or experience derived through the senses, which constantly undergo changes and modifications and thus fail to provide definite and unchanging standards of morality. Instead, it provides us with an objective source, the Divine revelation, as embodied in the Book of God and the Sunnah (way of life) of the Prophet, blessings and peace be on him. This source prescribes a standard of moral conduct that is permanent and universal and holds good in every age and under all circumstances.

The moral code of Islam ranges from smallest details of domestic life to the field of national and international behaviour. It guides us at every stage in life and makes us free from exclusive dependence on other sources of knowledge, although we may, of course, use these as an aid to this primary source.

Sanction Behind Morality

This concept of the universe and of man's place in it also provides the sanction that must lie at the back of every moral law, that is, the love and fear of God, the sense of accountability on the Day of Judgement and the promise of eternal bliss and reward in the Hereafter. Although Islam aims to cultivate a mass ethos which may induce individuals and groups to observe the principles of morality it lays down as well as helps the evolution of a political system which will enforce the moral law through its legislative and executive powers, Islam's moral law does not really depend on these external factors. It relies on the inherent desire for good in every man which is derived from belief in God and the Day of Judgement. Before laying down any moral injunctions, Islam seeks to implant firmly in man's heart the conviction that his dealings are with God, who sees him at all times and in all places; that he may hide himself from the whole world but not from God; that he may deceive everyone but God; that he can flee from the power of any person but not from God; that while the world can see only man's outward life, God knows his innermost intentions and desires; that while man may, in his short sojourn on earth, do whatever he likes, he has to die one day and present himself before the Divine court of justice where no special pleading or deception will be of any avail and where his future will be decided with complete impartiality. It is this belief in accountability to God which is the real force behind the moral law of Islam. If public opinion and the powers of the state give it support, so much the better; otherwise, this faith alone can keep a Muslim individual and a Muslim community on the straight path of virtue.

Motives and Incentives

The fact that a man *voluntarily and willingly* accepts God as his Creator and obedience to God as the aim of his life and strives to seek His pleasure in his every action provides sufficient incentive to obey the commandments which he believes to be from God. Belief that whoever obeys the Divine commands is sure to be rewarded in the Hereafter, whatever difficulties he may have to face in his life on earth, is another strong incentive for leading a virtuous life. And the belief that breaking the commandments of God will mean eternal punishment is an effective deterrent against violation of the moral law, however tempted a man may be by the superficial attractiveness of a certain course of action. If this hope and fear are firmly ingrained in one's heart, they will inspire virtuous deeds even on occasions when the immediate consequences may appear to be very damaging, and they will keep one away from evil even when it looks extremely attractive and profitable.

This clearly indicates that Islam possesses a distinctive criterion of good and evil, its own source of moral law, and its own sanctions and motivating force; through them it shapes the generally recognised moral virtues in all spheres of life into a balanced and comprehensive scheme and ensures that they are followed. It can therefore be justifiably claimed that Islam possesses a perfect moral system of its own. This system has many distinguishing features and I shall refer to three of the most significant ones which, in my opinion, form its special contribution to ethics.

Distinctive Features

1 By setting Divine pleasure as the objective of man's life, Islam has set the highest possible standard of morality, providing boundless possibilities for the moral evolution of humanity. By making Divine revelation the primary source of knowledge, it gives permanence and stability to moral standards, while at the same time allowing scope for reasonable flexibility and adjustment, though not for perversions or moral laxity. The love and fear of God become the real motives, which impel man to obey the moral law without external pressures. And through belief in God and the Day of Judgement, we are motivated to behave morally with earnestness and sincerity.

2 The Islamic moral order does not, through a mistaken love of originality and innovation, seek to lay down any new moral standards; nor does it seek to minimise the importance of the well-known moral standards, or give exaggerated importance to some and neglect others without cause. It takes all the recognised morals and assigns a suitable role to each within the total scheme of life. It widens the scope of their application to cover every aspect of man's private and social life – his domestic associations, his civic conduct, and his activities in the political, economic, legal and educational fields. It covers his life at home and in society, literally from the cradle to the grave. No sphere of life is exempt from the universal and comprehensive application of the moral principles of Islam. These ensure that the affairs of life, instead of being dominated by selfish desires and petty interests, are regulated by the dictates of morality.

3 The Islamic moral order guarantees for man a system of life which is free from all evil. It calls on the people not only to practise virtue, but also to eradicate vice. Those who respond to this call are gathered together into a community (Ummah) and given the name 'Muslims'. The main purpose underlying the formation of this community is that it should make an organised effort to establish and enforce goodness and suppress and eradicate evil.[10] It would be a day of mourning for this community and a bad day for the entire world if its efforts were at any time directed towards establishing evil and suppressing good.

27

3

Essential Features of the Islamic Political System

The political system of Islam is based on three principles: *Tawḥīd* (unity of God), *Risālat* (prophethood) and *Khilāfat* (vicegerency). It is difficult to appreciate the different aspects of Islamic polity without fully understanding these three principles. I will therefore begin with a brief exposition of what they are.[1]

Tawḥīd means that only God is the Creator, Sustainer and Master of the universe and of all that exists in it – organic or inorganic. The sovereignty of this kingdom is vested only in Him. He alone has the right to command or forbid. Worship and obedience are due to Him alone, no one and nothing else shares it in any way. Life, in all its forms, our physical organs and faculties, the apparent control which we have over nearly everything in our lives and the things themselves – none of them has been created or acquired by us in our own right. They have been bestowed on us entirely by God. Hence, it is not for us to decide the aim and purpose of our existence or to set the limits of our authority; nor is anyone else entitled to make these decisions for us. This right rests only with God, who has created us, endowed us with mental and physical faculties, and provided material things for our use.[2]

This principle of the unity of God totally negates the concept of the legal and political independence of human beings individually or collectively. No individual, family,

This is a new and revised translation of a talk given by the author on Radio Pakistan, Lahore, on 20th January, 1948.

class or race can set themselves above God. God alone is the Ruler and His commandments are the Law.[3]

The medium through which we receive the law of God is known as *Risālat*. We have received two things from this source: the Book in which God has set out His law, and the authoritative interpretation and exemplification of the Book by the Prophet, blessings and peace be on him, through word and deed, in his capacity as the representative of God. The Prophet, blessings and peace be on him, has also, in accordance with the intention of the Divine Book, given us a model for the Islamic way of life by himself implementing the law and providing necessary details where required. The combination of these two elements is called the Shari'ah.[4]

Now consider *Khilāfat*. According to the Arabic lexicon, it means 'representation'. Man, according to Islam, is the representative of God on earth, His vicegerent. That is to say, by virtue of the powers delegated to him by God, he is required to exercise his God-given authority in this world within the limits prescribed by God.

Take, for example, the case of an estate which someone has been appointed to administer on your behalf. You will see that four conditions are invariably met. First, the real ownership of the estate remains vested in you and not in the administrator; second, he administers your property only in accordance with your instructions; third, he exercises his authority within the limits prescribed by you; and fourth, in the administration of the trust he executes your will and not his own. These four conditions are so inherent in the concept of 'representation' that if any representative fails to observe them he will rightly be blamed for breaking the covenant which was implied in the concept of 'representation'. This is exactly what Islam means when it affirms that man is the vicegerent of God on earth. Hence, these four conditions are also involved in the concept of *Khilāfat*.[5]

A state that is established in accordance with this political theory will in fact be a human caliphate under the sovereignty of God and will do God's will by working within the limits prescribed by Him and in accordance with His instructions and injunctions.

Democracy in Islam

The above explanation of the term *Khilāfat* also makes it abundantly clear that no individual or dynasty or class can be *Khalīfah*, but that the authority of caliphate is bestowed on any community which accepts the principles of *Tawḥīd* and *Risālat*. In such a society, each individual shares the God-given caliphate. This is the point where democracy begins in Islam.

Every person in an Islamic society enjoys the rights and powers of the caliphate of God and in this respect all individuals are equal. No one can deprive anyone of his rights and powers. The agency for running the affairs of the state will be established in accordance with the will of these individuals, and the authority of the state will only be an extension of the powers of the individual delegated to it. Their opinion will be decisive in the formation of the Government, which will be run with their advice and in accordance with their wishes. Whoever gains their confidence will carry out the duties of the caliphate on their behalf; and when he loses this confidence he will have to relinquish his office. In this respect the political system in Islam is as perfect a democracy as ever can be.[6]

What distinguishes Islamic democracy from Western democracy is that while the latter is based on the concept of popular sovereignty the former rests on the principle of popular *Khilāfat*. In Western democracy the people are sovereign, in Islam sovereignty is vested in God and the people are His caliphs or representatives. In the former the people make their own laws; in the latter they have to follow and obey the laws (Shari‘ah) given by God through His Prophet. In one the Government undertakes to fulfil the will of the people; in the other the Government and the people alike have to do the will of God. Western democracy is a kind of absolute authority which exercises its powers in a free and uncontrolled manner, whereas Islamic democracy is subservient to the Divine Law and exercises its authority in accordance with the injunctions of God and within the limits prescribed by Him.

Purpose of the Islamic State

The Holy Qur'ān clearly states that the aim and purpose of this state, built on the foundation of *Tawḥīd*, *Risālat* and *Khilāfat*,[7] is the establishment, maintenance and development of those virtues which the Creator of the universe wishes human life to be enriched by, and the prevention and eradication of those evils which are abhorrent to God. The state in Islam is not intended for political administration only nor for the fulfilment through it of the collective will of any particular set of people. Rather, Islam places a high ideal before the state for the achievement of which it must use all the means at its disposal. The aim is to encourage the qualities of purity, beauty, goodness, virtue, success and prosperity which God wants to flourish in the life of His people and to suppress all kinds of exploitation and injustice. As well as placing before us this high ideal, Islam clearly states the desired virtues and the undesirable evils. The Islamic state can thus plan its welfare programmes in every age and in any environment.[8]

The constant demand made by Islam is that the principles of morality must be observed at all costs and in all walks of life. Hence, it lays down an unalterable requirement for the state to base its politics on justice, truth and honesty. It is not prepared, under any circumstances, to tolerate fraud, falsehood and injustice for the sake of political, administrative or national expediency. Whether it be relations between the rulers and the ruled within the state, or relations of the state with other states, precedence must always be given to truth, honesty and justice. It imposes obligations on the state similar to those it imposes on the individual: to fulfil all contracts and obligations; to have consistent standards in all dealings; to remember obligations as well as rights and not to forget the rights of others when expecting them to fulfil their obligations; to use power and authority for the establishment of justice and not for the perpetration of injustice; to look on duty as a sacred obligation; and to regard power as a trust from God to be used in the belief that one has to render an account of one's actions to Him in the Hereafter.[9]

Fundamental Rights

Although an Islamic state may be set up anywhere on earth, Islam does not seek to restrict human rights or privileges to the geographical limits of its own state. Islam has laid down universal fundamental rights[10] for humanity as a whole, which are to be observed and respected in all circumstances irrespective of whether a person lives on the territory of the Islamic state or outside it and whether he is at peace with the state or at war. For example, human blood is sacred and may not be spilled without justification; it is not permissible to oppress women, children, old people, the sick or the wounded; woman's honour and chastity must be respected in all circumstances; and the hungry must be fed, the naked clothed, and the wounded or diseased treated medically.

These, and a few other provisions, have been laid down by Islam as fundamental rights for every man by virtue of his status as a human being, to be enjoyed under the constitution of an Islamic state.

The rights of citizenship in Islam, however, are not confined to persons born within the limits of its state but are granted to every Muslim irrespective of his place of birth. A Muslim *ipso facto* becomes the citizen of an Islamic state as soon as he sets foot on its territory with the intention of living there; he thus enjoys equal rights of citizenship with those who are its citizens by birth. Citizenship must therefore be common to all the citizens of all the Islamic states that exist in the world; a Muslim will not need a passport for entry or exit from any of them.[11] And every Muslim must be regarded as eligible for positions of the highest responsibility in an Islamic state without distinction of race, colour or class.[12]

Islam has also laid down certain rights for non-Muslims who may be living within the boundaries of an Islamic state, and these rights must necessarily form part of the Islamic constitution.[13] According to Islamic terminology such non-Muslims are called *dhimmīs* (the covenanted), implying that the Islamic state has entered into a covenant with them and guaranteed their rights.

The life, property and honour of a *dhimmī* is to be respected and protected in exactly the same way as that of a

33

Muslim citizen. There is no difference between Muslim and non-Muslim citizens in respect of civil or criminal law; and the Islamic state shall not interfere with the personal law of non-Muslims. They will have full freedom of conscience and belief and will be entitled to perform their religious rites and ceremonies. As well as being able to practise their religion, they are entitled to criticise Islam. However the rights given in this respect are not unlimited: the civil law of the country has to be fully respected and all criticism has to be made within its framework.

These rights are irrevocable and non-Muslims can only be deprived of them if they renounce the covenant which grants them citizenship. However much a non-Muslim state may oppress its Muslim citizens, it is not permissible for an Islamic state to retaliate against its non-Muslim subjects. This injunction holds good even if all the Muslims outside the boundaries of an Islamic state are massacred.

Executive and Legislature

The responsibility for the administration of the Government in an Islamic state is entrusted to an Amir (leader) who may be likened to the President or the Prime Minister in a Western democratic state. All adult men and women who accept the fundamentals of the constitution are entitled to vote in the election for the leader.[14]

The basic qualifications for the election of an Amir are that he should command the confidence of the largest number of people in respect of his knowledge and grasp of the spirit of Islam; he should possess the Islamic attribute of fear of God; he should be endowed with the quality of statesmanship. In short, he should be both able and virtuous.

A *Shūrā* (consultative council), elected by the people, will assist and guide the Amir. It is obligatory for the Amir to administer the country with the advice of his *Shūrā*. The Amir can retain office only so long as he enjoys the confidence of the people, and must resign when he loses this confidence. Every citizei. has the right to criticise the Amir and his Government, and all reasonable means for the expression of public opinion should be available.

Legislation in an Islamic state should be within the limits prescribed by the Shari'ah. The injunctions of God and His Prophet are to be accepted and obeyed and no legislative body can alter or modify them or make any new laws which are contrary to their spirit. The duty of ascertaining the real intent of those commandments which are open to more than one interpretation should devolve on people possessing a specialised knowledge of the law of Shari'ah. Hence, such matters may have to be referred to a sub-committee of the *Shūrā* comprising men learned in Islamic law. Great scope would still be available for legislation on questions not covered by any specific injunctions of the Shari'ah, and the advisory council or legislature is free to legislate in regard to these matters.

In Islam the judiciary is not placed under the control of the executive. It derives its authority directly from the Shari'ah and is answerable to God. The judges will obviously be appointed by the Government but, once appointed, will have to administer justice impartially according to the law of God. All the organs and functionaries of the Government should come within their jurisdiction: even the highest executive authority of the Government will be liable to be called upon to appear in a court of law as a plaintiff or defendant. Rulers and ruled are subject to the same law and there can be no discrimination on the basis of position, power or privilege. Islam stands for equality and scrupulously adheres to this principle in the social, economic and political realms alike.

4

The Islamic Social Order

The foundations of the social system of Islam rest on the belief that all human beings are equal and constitute one single fraternity.[1]

Equality of Mankind

God created a human couple to herald the beginning of the life of mankind on earth, and everybody living in the world today originates from this couple. The progeny of this couple were initially a single group with one religion and the same language. But as their numbers gradually increased, they spread all over the earth and, as a natural result of their diversification and growth, were divided into various tribes and nationalities. They came to speak different languages; their modes of dress varied; and their ways of living also differed widely. Climates and environments affected their colour and physical features. All these differences exist in the world of reality and Islam does not seek to ignore them. But it disapproves of the prejudices which have arisen among mankind because of these differences in race, colour, language and nationality. Islam makes clear to all men that they have come from the same parents and are therefore brothers and equal as human beings.[2]

Islam says that if there *is* any real difference between man and man it cannot be one of race, colour, country or language,

This is a new and revised translation of a talk given by the author on Radio Pakistan, Lahore, on 10th February, 1948.

but of ideas, beliefs and principles. Two children of the same mother, though they may be equal from the point of view of a common ancestry, will have to go their different ways in life if their beliefs and moral conduct differ. On the contrary, two people, one in the East and the other in the West, even though geographically and outwardly separated by vast distances, will tread the same path in life if they share the same code of moral behaviour. On the basis of this fundamental tenet, Islam seeks to build a principled and ideological society very different from the racial, nationalistic and parochial societies existing in the world today.

The basis of co-operative effort among men in such a society is not the place of one's birth but a creed and a moral principle. Anyone, if he believes in God as his Master and Lord and accepts the guidance of the Prophets as the law of his life, can join this community, whether he is a resident of America or Africa, whether he belongs to the Semitic race or the Aryan, whether he is black or fair-skinned, whether he speaks a European language or Arabic. All those who join this community will have the same rights and social status. They will not be subjected to any racial, national or class distinctions. No one will be regarded as high or low. There will be no untouchability. There will be no special restrictions upon them in making marriages, eating and drinking and social contacts. No one will be looked down upon because of his birth or work. No one will claim any distinctive rights by virtue of his caste, community or ancestry. Man's merit will not depend on his family connections or riches, but only on whether he is better than others in moral conduct or excels others in piety and righteousness.[3]

Such social order, transcending as it does geographical boundaries and the barriers of race, colour and language, is appropriate for all parts of the world; on its foundations can be raised the universal brotherhood of man. In societies based on race or nationality only those people can join who belong to a particular race or nation, but in Islam anyone who accepts its creed and moral standards can become a member, possessing equal rights with everyone else. Those who do not accept this creed, while obviously not being received into the community, are treated with tolerance and humanity and guaranteed all the basic human rights.

It is clear that if two children of the same mother differ in their ideas, their ways of life will be different; but this does not mean that they cease to be brothers. In the same way, if two nations or two groups of people living in the same country differ in their fundamental beliefs, principles and ideology, their societies will also certainly differ; yet they will continue to share the common ties of humanity. Hence, the Islamic society offers to non-Muslim societies and groups the maximum social and cultural rights that can possibly be accorded.

Institution of the Family[3]

The foremost and fundamental institution of human society is the family unit. A family is established by the coming together of a man and a woman, and their contact brings into existence a new generation. This then produces ties of kinship and community, which, in turn, gradually develop further ties. The family is an instrument of continuity which prepares the succeeding generation to serve human civilisation and to discharge its social obligations with devotion, sincerity and enthusiasm. This institution does not merely recruit cadets for the maintenance of human culture, but positively desires that those who are to come will be better members of society. In this respect the family can be truly called the source of the progress, development, prosperity and strength of human civilisation.[4] Islam therefore devotes much attention to the issues relating to the family and strives to establish it on the healthiest and strongest possible foundations.

According to Islam the correct relationship between man and woman is marriage, a relationship in which social responsibilities are fully accepted and which results in the emergence of a family. Sexual permissiveness and other similar types of irresponsible behaviour are not dismissed by Islam as mere innocent pastimes or ordinary transgressions. Rather, they are acts which strike at the very roots of society. Hence, Islam holds all extra-marital sex as sinful and forbidden (*ḥarām*) and makes it a criminal offence. Severe punishments are prescribed to deter would-be offenders.[5]

39

Purdah, which regulates the free association of men and women, restrictions on erotic music and obscene pictures and the discouragement of the spread of all forms of pornography, are other weapons used in the fight to protect and strengthen the institution of the family.[6]

Islam does not look on adult celibacy simply with disfavour – it calls on every young man to take upon himself the social responsibilities of married life just as his parents did in their time. Nor does Islam regard asceticism and lifelong celibacy merely as being of no benefit; it sees them as departures from the nature of man and as acts of revolt against the Divine scheme of things.[7]

It also strongly disapproves of those rites, ceremonies or restrictions which tend to make marriage a difficult affair. Islam tries to make marriage the easiest and fornication the most difficult thing in society – and not vice versa as it is in most societies today. Hence, after debarring certain blood relatives from entering into matrimony with one another, it has legalised marriage with all other near and distant kith and kin. It has removed all distinctions of caste and community, and permitted matrimony of any Muslim with any other Muslim. It has urged that the *mehr* (dower) should be fixed at a figure which can be easily borne by both sides. It has dispensed with the necessity of priests and register offices. In an Islamic society marriage is a plain and simple ceremony which can be performed anywhere before two witnesses, though it is essential that the proceedings should not be kept secret. Society must know that the couple are now going to live as husband and wife.

Within the family itself Islam has assigned to the man a position of authority so that he can maintain order and discipline as the head of the household. Islam expects the wife to obey her husband and look after his well-being; and it expects the children to behave accordingly to their parents. Islam does not favour a loose and disjointed family system devoid of proper authority, control and discipline. Discipline can only be maintained through a central authority and, in the view of Islam, the position of father in the family is such that it makes him the fittest person to have this responsibility.[8]

But this does not mean that man has been made a house-

40

hold tyrant and woman has been handed over to him as a helpless chattel. According to Islam the real spirit of marital life is love, understanding and mutual respect. If woman has been asked to obey her husband, the latter has been called on to treat the wife with love, affection and sweetness and to make the welfare of his family his top priority.[9]

Although Islam places great emphasis on the marital bond, it only wants it to remain intact as long as it is founded on the sweetness of love or there exists at least the possibility of lasting companionship. If neither of these two conditions obtain, it gives man the right of divorce and woman the right of separation; and under certain conditions, where married life has become a source of misery, the Islamic courts of justice have the authority to annul the marriage.

Relatives and Neighbours

After the limited circle of the family, the next social sphere is that of kinship and blood relationship. Islam wants all those who are related through common parents, common brothers and sisters or marriage to be affectionate, co-operative and helpful to each other. In many places in the Qur'ān good treatment of the near relations (*Dhawī-al-qurbā*) is enjoined.[10] In the Hadith of the Prophet, blessings and peace be on him, proper treatment of one's blood relations has been strongly emphasised and counted among the highest virtues. A person who cold-shoulders his relations or treats them indifferently is looked on by Islam with great disfavour.[11]

But this does not mean that it is an Islamic virtue to favour one's relations. If such support or bias towards one's relations results in injustice, it is repugnant to Islam, and is condemned as an act of *Jāhiliyyah* (ignorance). Similarly, it is utterly against the principles of Islam for a government official or public servant to support his relations at public expense or to favour his kith and kin in his official decisions: this would actually be a sinful act. Fair treatment of one's relations, as enjoined by Islam, should be at one's own expense and within the limits of justice and fair-play.

41

After relations come one's neighbours. The Qur'ān has divided them into three categories: a neighbour who is also a relation; a neighbour who is a stranger; and a casual or temporary neighbour with whom one happens to live or travel for a certain time.[12] All of them are deserving of sympathy, affection, kindness and fair treatment. The Prophet, blessings and peace be on him, once said that the rights of the neighbour were so strongly emphasised by the angel Gabriel that he thought neighbours might even share one's inheritance. (*Bukhārī* and *Muslim*)

In one Hadith the Prophet, blessings and peace be on him, said: Anyone whose neighbour is not safe from his misdeeds is not a true Believer. (*Bukhārī* and *Muslim*) Again, he said: A person who enjoys a meal while his neighbour is starving is not a true Believer. (*Aḥmad, Baihaqī*). The Prophet, blessings and peace be on him, was once asked about the fate of a woman who performed many Prayers and fasted extensively and who was a frequent almsgiver, but whose neighbours complained of her abusive tongue. He said: Such a woman shall be in the Hell-fire. He was, then, asked about another woman who did not possess these virtues but did not trouble her neighbours either, and he said: She would be in Paradise. (*Aḥmad, Baihaqī*) The Prophet, blessings and peace be on him, has laid so much emphasis on being considerate to neighbours that he has advised that whenever a Muslim brings home fruit for his children he should either send some to his neighbours as a gift, or at least take care not to offend them by throwing the peelings away outside their door.[13] On another occasion he said: A man is really good if his neighbours regard him as such, and bad if they consider him so. (*Ibn Māiah*)

Islam, therefore, requires all neighbours to be loving and helpful and to share each other's sorrows and happiness. It enjoins them to establish social relations in which one can depend upon the other and regard his life, honour and property safe among his neighbours. A society in which two people. separated only by a wall, remain unacquainted with one another for years, and in which those living in the same area of a town have no interest or trust in one another, can never be called Islamic.

Next to these come the wider relationships covering the whole of society. The broad principles on which Islam wants people to structure their social lives are:

> To co-operate in acts of goodness and righteousness and not to co-operate in acts of sin and injustice. (al-Mā'idah 5: 2)

> One's friendship should be only for seeking the pleasure of God: whatever you give should be given because God likes it to be given, and whatever you withhold should be withheld because God wishes so. (*Tirmidhī*)

> You are the best community ever raised among mankind; your duty is to command people to do good and prevent them from committing evil. (Al 'Imrān 3: 110)

> Do not think evil of each other, nor probe into each other's affairs, nor incite one against the other. Avoid hatred and jealousy. Do not unnecessarily oppose each other. Always remain the slaves of Allah, and live as brothers to each other. (*Muslim*)

> Do not help a tyrant, knowing him to be such. (*Abū Dā'ūd*)

> To support the community when it is in the wrong is like falling into a well while catching the tail of your camel which was about to fall into it. (*Abū Dā'ūd; Mishkāwt*)

> No one among you shall be a true Believer unless he likes for others what he likes for himself. (*Bukhārī* and *Muslim*)

5

The Economic Principles of Islam

Islam has laid down certain principles and limits for the economic activity of man so that the entire pattern of production, exchange and distribution of wealth may conform to the Islamic standard of justice and equity. Islam does not concern itself with time-bound methods and techniques of economic production or with the details of organisational patterns and mechanisms. Such methods are specific to every age and are evolved in accordance with the needs and requirements of the community and the exigencies of the economic situation. Islam's concern is that whatever the particular form of economic activity in operation, its underlying principles should always be the same.[1]

According to the Islamic point of view, God has created for mankind the earth and all that it contains. It is, therefore, the birthright of every human being to try to secure his share of the world's wealth and sustenance.[2] Islam does not allow a particular person, class, race or group of people to create a monopoly in certain economic activities: equal opportunities for all is its watchword.

Right of Property

Resources which are provided by nature and which can be used directly by man may be utilised freely, and everyone is

This is a new and revised translation of a talk given by the author on Radio Pakistan, Lahore, on 2nd March, 1948.

entitled to benefit from them according to his needs. Water in the rivers and springs, timber in the forests, fruits of wild plants, wild grass and fodder, air, animals of the jungle, minerals under the surface of the earth and similar other resources cannot be monopolised by anyone nor can restrictions of any sort be imposed on their free use by God's creatures to fulfil their own needs.[3] Of course, people who want to use any of these things for commercial purposes can be required to pay taxes to the state. Or, if there is misuse of the resources, the Government may intervene. But there is nothing to prevent individuals availing themselves of God's earth as long as they do not interfere with the rights of others or of the state.

It is not right that things created by God for the benefit of mankind should be taken possession of, and then kept idle and useless. One should either benefit from them oneself, or make them available to others. On the basis of this principle Islam holds that no one can keep his land unused for more than three years. If, during this period, he does not himself use it for cultivation or for construction of buildings or for some other purpose, such land shall be treated as 'vacated', and anyone else who makes use of it shall not be liable to be proceeded against in law, nor shall the Government have any authority to hand it over to someone else (including the previous owner).[4]

Anyone who takes possession of the earth's natural resources and puts them to good use acquires a rightful title over them. For instance, if somebody takes possession of an uncultivated piece of land, on which nobody has a prior right of ownership, and makes productive use of it, he cannot be arbitrarily dispossessed of that piece of land.[5]

This is how every right of ownership originated in the world. When man first appeared, everything was available to everyone, and whoever took possession of anything and made it useful in any manner became its owner; that is to say, he acquired the right to use it specifically for his own purpose and to obtain compensation from others if they wanted to use it. This is the natural basis of all the economic activity of mankind.

The rights of ownership are to be honoured, though it is always open to ascertain if a particular ownership is legally valid or not. Islam cannot approve of economic policies which destroy the rights conferred by the Shari'ah, however attractive their names may be and whatever welfare pretensions they may make. Social justice and collective good are very dear to Islam, but in their name the rights given by the Shari'ah cannot be trampled. It is as unjust to reduce or remove the restrictions placed by the Shari'ah, for the sake of the good of the community as a whole, on the rights of individual ownership as it is to add restrictions and limitations on them which do not fit into the Shari'ah.[6] It is one of the duties of an Islamic state to protect the legal rights of individuals and, at the same time to compel them to fulfil their obligations to the community as enjoined by law. That is how Islam strikes a balance between individualism and collectivism.

The Problem of Equality

God has not distributed His gifts and favours equally among mankind but, in His infinite wisdom, has given some individuals more than others. Just as this is true of pleasantness of voice, excellence of physique and intellectual power and so on, so, too, is it the case with the material conditions of life. Human existence has been so ordained that divergence, variety and inequality among men in their ways and standards of living seems to be natural. Variety is the spice of life, and the driving spirit behind human endeavour and excellence.[7]

Consequently, all those ideologies which want to force an artificial economic equality on mankind are mistaken, unrealistic and impossible to realise. The equality which Islam believes in is equality of opportunity to secure a livelihood and to climb the ladder of success and prosperity. Islam desires that no obstacles should exist in society to prevent an individual from striving for a living according to his capacity and talents; nor should any social distinctions exist with the object of safeguarding the privileges of a certain class, race, dynasty or group of people.

All those ideologies which serve vested interests, or which seek to perpetuate the power of a certain group, are also repugnant to Islam and can have no place in its scheme of things. Such movements seek to establish, through force if necessary, an *unnatural inequality* in place of the natural limited inequality which provides incentive to effort in society. At the same time, Islam does not agree with those who want to enforce complete equality in respect of the means of production and the fruits of economic endeavour, as they aim at replacing limited natural inequality by an artificial equality.

Only that system can be the nearest to human nature in which everyone joins the economic struggle at his own level and in the circumstances in which God has created him. He who has inherited an aeroplane should make use of it; while he who has only a pair of legs should stand on his feet and try to improve his lot. The laws of society should neither be such as would establish a permanent monopoly for the aeroplane-owner (over his aeroplane) and make it impossible for the bare-footed to acquire an aeroplane nor such that the race for everyone should compulsorily begin from the same point and under the same conditions so that they would all be tied to each other right till the end of the race. On the contrary, economic laws should be such as to make it possible for the bare-footed, who started his race under adverse conditions, to possess an aeroplane, if he can do so by dint of his effort and ability, and for he who inherited the aeroplane to be left behind in the race and to lose it, if he does not have the ability or efficiency to keep it. Effort should be rewarded and laziness penalised.

Social Justice

Islam does not want this economic race to take place in an atmosphere of moral neutrality and social apathy. The participants should be just and kind to one another. Islam, through its moral injunctions, aims at creating a feeling of mutual love and affection among people, through which they may help their weak and weary brethren, and at the same time create a permanent institution in society to guarantee assistance to those who lack the necessary means and abilities to

48

succeed. People who are unable to take part in the economic race and those who need help to get started in it should receive their share of the blessings of life from this social institution.[8]

To this end Islam has commanded that Zakāt should be levied at the rate of two and a half percent per annum on the total accumulated wealth [of each individual] in the country, as well as on invested capital; five percent or ten percent, depending on the method of watering, should be collected on agricultural produce; and twenty percent on certain mineral products. The annual Zakāt should also be levied, at a specified rate, on cattle owned by anyone who has more than a certain minimum number. The amount of Zakāt thus collected is to be spent on the poor, the orphans and the needy.

This system provides a means of social insurance whereby everyone in an Islamic society is provided with at least the necessities of life. No worker can ever be forced, through fear of starvation, to accept conditions of employment which may be unfairly imposed on him by his employer. And nobody's physical health is allowed to deteriorate for lack of proper medical care and hospitalisation.

Islam aims at striking a balance between the individual and the community, which will promote individual freedom and at the same time ensure that such freedom is positively conducive to the growth and tranquility of the community as a whole. Islam does not approve of a political or economic organisation which aims at submerging the identity of the individual beneath that of the community, and depriving him of the freedom essential for the proper development of his personality and talent. The inevitable consequence of nationalising a country's means of production is the annihilation of the individual by the community; in these circumstances the existence and development of his individuality becomes extremely difficult, if not impossible.

Just as political and social freedom is essential for the individual, economic freedom is necessary for a civilised moral existence. Unless we desire to eliminate completely the individuality of man, our social life must have enough freedom for an individual to be able to earn his living, to maintain the integrity of his conscience and to develop his moral and intellectual faculties according to his own inclinations and aptitudes. Living on the dole or on charity at the hands of others cannot be very satisfying, even if the sums involved are generous: the retardation of mental, moral and spiritual development which it ultimately leads to can never be counteracted by mere physical welfare and prosperity.

Nor does Islam favour a system of unbridled economic and social freedom which gives individuals a blank cheque to achieve their objectives at the possible cost of the good of the community as a whole, or which enables them to misappropriate the wealth of others. Between these two extremes, Islam has adopted the middle course according to which the individual is first called upon, in the interest of the community, to accept certain restrictions, and is then left free to regulate his own affairs. He has freedom of enterprise and competition within a framework which guarantees the good of both the individual and society. It is not possible to explain all these obligations and restrictions in detail and I shall, therefore, content myself with presenting a bare outline of them.

Obligations and Restrictions

Take first the example of earning a living. The meticulous care with which Islam has distinguished between right and wrong in respect of the means of earning wealth is not to be found in any other legal and social system. It condemns as illegal all those means of livelihood which injure, morally or materially, the interests of another individual or of society as a whole. Islamic law categorically rejects as illegal the manufacture and sale of liquor and other intoxicants, adultery, professional dancing, gambling, transactions of a speculative or fraudulent nature, transactions in which the gain of one party is absolutely guaranteed while that of the other party is left uncertain and doubtful, and price manipulation by withholding the sale of the necessities of life.[9]

If we examine this aspect of the economic laws of Islam, we will find a long list of practices declared illegal, most of which can and are making people millionaires in the capitalist system. Islam forbids all these by law, and allows freedom of earning wealth only by those means through which a person renders some real and useful service to the community and thereby entitles himself to fair and just compensation for it.

Islam accepts the right of ownership of an individual over the wealth earned by him by legitimate means; but these rights are not unrestrained. A man can only spend his legitimate wealth in certain specified ways. He may not waste his riches on idle luxury, nor may he use his wealth to behave arrogantly towards his fellows. Certain forms of wasteful expenditure have been unequivocally prohibited while some others, though not expressly banned, may be prohibited at the discretion of an Islamic Government.[10]

One is permitted to accumulate wealth that is left over after meeting one's legitimate and reasonable commitments and these savings can also be used to produce more wealth; there are, however, restrictions on both these activities. A rich man will, of course, have to pay Zakāt at the rate of two and a half percent a year on the accumulation exceeding the specified minimum. He can only invest it in a business which has been declared legitimate. In this connection, he may own the legitimate business himself or he may make his capital available to others on a profit-loss sharing basis.

It is not at all objectionable in Islam if, working within these limits, a man becomes a millionaire; rather, this will constitute a Divine favour. But in the interests of the community as a whole, Islam imposes two conditions on the individual: first, that he should pay Zakāt on his commercial goods and 'Ushr (one tenth) on the value of agricultural produce; second, that he should deal fairly and honestly with those he does business with in trade, industry or agriculture, with those he employs and with the Government and the community at large. If he does not voluntarily act justly to others, particularly his employees, the Islamic state will compel him to do so.

Even wealth that is accumulated within these legal limits is not allowed by Islam to be concentrated at one point or in one place for a long time. Through its law of inheritance Islam spreads it among a large number of people from generation to generation.[11] In this respect the Islamic law is different from that of other inheritance laws; most of them attempt to keep the wealth once accumulated by a person concentrated in the

51

hands of one main beneficiary from generation to generation. In Islam, wealth accumulated by a person in his lifetime is distributed among all of his near relatives soon after his death. If there are no near relatives, distant relatives benefit from it in the proportions laid down by the law for each one of them. And if no distant relative is forthcoming, then the entire Muslim society is entitled to share in the inheritance. Under this law the creation or continuance of any big family of capitalists or landlords becomes impossible.

6

The Spiritual Path in Islam

What is the spiritual path in Islam and what is its place in the life as a whole? To answer this it is necessary to study carefully the difference between the Islamic concept of spirituality and that of other religions and ideologies. Without a clear understanding of this difference it often happens that, when talking about the spirituality in Islam, many of the vague notions associated with the word 'spiritual' unconsciously come to mind; it then becomes difficult for one to comprehend that this spirituality of Islam not only transcends the dualism of spirit and matter but is the nucleus of its integrated and unified concept of life.

Body-Soul Conflict

The idea which has influenced most the climate of philosophical and religious thought is that body and soul are mutually antagonistic, and can develop only at each other's expense. For the soul, the body is a prison and the activities of daily life are the shackles which keep it in bondage and arrest its growth. This has inevitably led to the universe being divided into the spiritual and the secular.

Those who chose the secular path were convinced that they could not meet the demands of spirituality, and thus they led highly material and hedonistic lives. All spheres of worldly activity, whether social, political, economic or cul-

This is a new and revised translation of a talk given by the author on Radio Pakistan, Lahore, on 16th March, 1948.

tural, were deprived of the light of spirituality: injustice and tyranny were the result.

Conversely, those who wanted to tread the path of spiritual excellence came to see themselves as 'noble outcasts' from the world. They believed that it was impossible for spiritual growth to be compatible with a 'normal' life. In their view physical self-denial and mortification of the flesh were necessary for the development and perfection of the spirit. They invented spiritual exercises and ascetic practices which killed physical desires and dulled the body's senses. They regarded forests, mountains and other solitary places as ideal for spiritual development because the hustle and bustle of life would not interfere with their meditations. They could not conceive of spiritual development except through withdrawal from the world.

This conflict of body and soul resulted in the evolution of two different ideals for the perfection of man. One was that man should be surrounded by all possible material comforts and regard himself as nothing but an animal. Men learnt to fly like birds, swim like fish, run like horses and even terrorise and destroy like wolves – but they did not learn how to live like noble human beings. The other was that the senses should be not only subdued and conquered but extra-sensory powers awakened and the limitations of the sensory world done away with. With these new conquests men would be able to hear distant voices like powerful wireless sets, see remote objects as one does with a telescope, and develop powers through which the mere touch of their hand or a passing glance would heal the unhealable.

The Islamic viewpoint differs radically from these approaches. According to Islam, God has appointed the human soul as His *Khalīfah* (vicegerent) in this world. He has invested it with a certain authority, and given it certain responsibilities and obligations for the fulfilment of which He has endowed it with the best and most suitable physical frame. The body has been created with the sole object of allowing the soul to use it in the exercise of its authority and the fulfilment of its duties and responsibilities. The body is not a prison for the soul, but its workshop or factory; and if the soul is to grow and develop, it is only through this workshop. Consequently, this world is not a place of punishment in which the human soul unfortunately finds itself, but a field in which God has sent it to work and do its duty towards Him.[1]

So spiritual development should not take the form of a man turning away from this workshop and retreating into a corner. Rather, man should live and work in it, and give the best account of himself that he can. It is in the nature of an examination for him; every aspect and sphere of life is, as it were, a question paper: the home, the family, the neighbourhood, the society, the market-place, the office, the factory, the school, the law courts, the police station, the parliament, the peace conference and the battlefield, all represent question papers which man has been called upon to answer. If he leaves most of the answer-books blank, he is bound to fail the examination. Success and development are only possible if man devotes his whole life to this examination and attempts to answer all the question papers he can.

Islam rejects and condemns the ascetic view of life, and proposes a set of methods and processes for the spiritual development of man, not outside this world but inside it. The real place for the growth of the spirit is in the midst of life and not in solitary places of spiritual hibernation.[2]

Criterion of Spiritual Development

We shall now discuss how Islam judges the development or decay of the soul. In his capacity as the vicegerent (*Khalīfah*) of God, man is answerable to Him for all his activities. It is his duty to use all the powers which he has been given in accordance with the Divine will. He should utilise to the fullest extent all the faculties and potentialities bestowed upon him for seeking God's approval. In his dealings with other people he should behave in such a way as to try to please God. In brief, all his energies should be directed towards regulating the affairs of this world in the way in which God wants them to be regulated. The better a man does this, with a sense of responsibility, obedience and humility, and with the object of seeking the pleasure of the Lord, the nearer will he be to God. In Islam, spiritual development is synonymous

55

with nearness to God. Similarly, he will not be able to get near to God if he is lazy and disobedient. And distance from God signifies, in Islam, the spiritual fall and decay of man.

From the Islamic point of view, therefore, the sphere of activity of the religious man and the secular man is the same. Not only will both work in the same spheres; the religious man will work with greater enthusiasm than the secular man. The man of religion will be as active as the man of the world – indeed, more active – in his domestic and social life, which extends from the confines of the household to the market square, and even to international conferences.

What *will* distinguish their actions will be the nature of their relationship with God and the aims behind their actions. Whatever a religious man does, will be done with the feeling that he is answerable to God, that he must try to secure Divine pleasure, that his actions must be in accordance with God's laws. A secular person will be indifferent towards God and will be guided in his actions only by his personal motives. This difference makes the whole of the material life of a man of religion a totally spiritual venture, and the whole of the life of a secular person an existence devoid of the spark of spirituality.

The Road to Spirituality

The first necessity for progression along the path of spiritual development is *īmān* (faith).[3] The mind and heart of a man should always be aware: God alone is His Master, Sovereign and Deity; seeking His pleasure is the aim of all his endeavours; and His commands alone are the commands that are to be obeyed. This should be a firm conviction, based not merely on the intellect, but also on acceptance by the will. The stronger and deeper this conviction, the more profound a man's faith will be.

The second stage is that of obedience (*itā'at*), meaning that man gives up his independence and accepts subservience to God. This subservience is called *īslām* (submission)[4] in the language of the Qur'ān. Thus, man should not only acknowledge God as his Lord and Sovereign but should actually submit before Him and fashion his entire life in obedience to Him.

The third stage is that of *taqwā* (God-consciousness).[5] It consists in a practical manifestation of one's faith in God in one's daily life. *Taqwā* also means desisting from everything which God has forbidden or has disapproved of; man must be in a state of readiness to undertake all that God has commanded and to observe the distinctions between lawful and unlawful, right and wrong, and good and bad in life

The last and the highest stage is that of *ihsān* (godliness).[6] It signifies that man has attained highest excellence in words, deeds and thoughts, identifying his will with the will of God and harmonising it, to the best of his knowledge and ability, with the Divine will. He thus begins to like what is liked by the Lord and to dislike what He dislikes. Man should then not only avoid evil, for it displeases his Lord, but should use all his powers to eradicate it from the face of the earth; he should not be content with adorning himself with the good which God wants to flourish but should also strive to attain and propagate it in the world, even at the cost of his life. A man who reaches this stage attains the highest pinnacle of spirituality and is nearest to God.[7]

This path of spiritual development is not meant for individuals only but for communities and nations as well. Like individuals, a community, after passing through the various stages of spiritual elevation may reach the ultimate stage of *ihsān*; a state also, through all its administrative machinery, may become *mu'min* (faithful), *muslim* (obedient), *muttaqī* (God-conscious) and *muhsin* (godly). In fact, the ideals aimed at by Islam are fully achieved only when the whole community accepts them and a *muttaqī* and *muhsin* state comes into existence. The highest form of civilisation, based on goodness, is then reached.

Let us now look at the mechanism of spiritual training which Islam has laid down to prepare individuals and society for this process.

The methods that Islam lays down for spiritual development rest, in addition, obviously, to faith (*īmān*), on five pillars.

The first is the Prayer (Ṣalāt), which brings man into communion with God five times a day, reviving his remembrance, reiterating his fear, developing his love, reminding

57

him of the Divine commands again and again, and thus preparing him for obedience to God. It is obligatory to offer some of these Prayers in Congregation as well so that the whole community and society may be prepared to journey on the path of spiritual development.[8]

The second is the Fast (Ṣawm), which for a full month every year trains each man individually, and the Muslim community as a whole, in righteousness and self-restraint; it enables society, the rich and the poor alike, to experience hunger, and prepares people to undergo any hardships in their search to please God.[9]

The third is the Almsgiving (Zakāt), which develops the sense of monetary sacrifice, sympathy and co-operation among Muslims. There are people who wrongly interpret Zakāt as a tax; in fact, the spirit underlying Zakāt is entirely different from that of a tax. The real meaning of Zakāt is sublimity and purification. By using this word, Islam seeks to impress on man the fact that, inspired by a true love of God, the monetary help which he renders to his brethren will uplift and purify his soul.[10]

The fourth is the Pilgrimage (Ḥajj), which aims at fostering that universal brotherhood of the faithful which is based on the worship of God, and which results in a worldwide movement that has been responding to the call of Truth throughout the centuries and will, God willing, go on answering this call till eternity.

The last is Jihad, that is, exerting oneself to the utmost to disseminate the word of God and to make it supreme, and to remove all the impediments to Islam – through tongue or . pen or sword. The aim is to live a life of dedication to the cause of Allah and, if necessary, to sacrifice one's life in the discharge of this mission. This is the highest spirituality, rooted in the real world, which Islam wants to cultivate. Life-affirmation based on goodness and piety, and not life-denial, is what Islam stands for. And this lends a unique character to Islam.[11]

NOTES

(contributed by Khurram Murad)

Chapter 1

1 According to Islam, Adam was the first Prophet of God on earth.

2 Mawdudi, *Tafhīmul Qur'ān*, Vol. I, Lahore, 1974, pp. 16–19.

3 The translator here has borrowed from the words of Shakespeare who has beautifully portrayed this attitude of man in the following lines:

> Man, proud man
> Direct in a little brief authority –
> Most ignorant of what he's most assured.
> His glossy essence – like an angry ape,
> Plays such fantastic tricks before heaven,
> As make the angels weep.

> *Measure for Measure* (Isabella), Act II, Sc. II – Shakespeare.

4 *Kalimah* is a statement of the profession of faith and one enters the fold of Islam by pronouncing it. The *Kalimah* is: 'There is no God but Allah, Muhammad is His Messenger.'

5 Mawdudi, *Tafhīmul Qur'ān*, Vol. II, Lahore, 1975, pp. 235–9.

6 This is how Sayyid Mawdudi put it:

> To follow this code of conduct is the truest and the most consistent attitude for mankind. It sets standards for the orderly behaviour of man both individually and collectively and in respect of the biggest as well as the smallest task he may have to face. Having once accepted the philosophy of life enunciated by The Book and The Messenger as the embodiment of Reality, one has no justification for not obeying God's

revealed Guidance in the sphere of one's choice also. This, for a host of reasons, is the most rational approach for man to follow. Firstly, the power and the organs through which our free-will functions, are gifts from God and not the result of our own efforts. Secondly, the independence of choice itself has been delegated to us by God and not won by us through our personal endeavour. Thirdly, all those things in which our free-will operates are not only the property but also the creation of God. Fourthly, the territory in which we exercise our independence and freedom is also the territory of God. Fifthly, the harmonisation of human life with the universe dictates the necessity of there being one Sovereign and a common source of Law for both spheres of human activity – the voluntary and the involuntary, or, in other words, the moral and the physical. The separation of these two spheres into water-tight compartments leads to the creation of an irreconcilable conflict which finally lands not only the individual but also the nation and the whole of humanity in endless trouble and disaster. Mawdudi, *Islamic Law and Constitution*, Lahore, 1960, p. 49.

7 Selections from *Islamic Law and Constitution*, ibid., pp. 46–54.

Chapter 2

1 This word is used in its wide sense, meaning the moral consciousness of man. It should not be taken in the limited sense in which it is used by writers in anthropological studies of the so-called evolution of morals.

2 Some anthropologists and sociologists may not fully subscribe to this view, but on deeper reflection it is found that despite superficial differences in mores and morals there is an essential element which is universal, existing from the very first day, particularly in the civilised phases of human existence. And it is these periods which the author has in view. The nature and causes of differences are discussed in the following paragraphs.

3 For a more detailed exposition by the author, see his *The Ethical Viewpoint of Islam*, Lahore, 1965.

4 For a review of the moral systems of the world, see ibid.

5 The Qur'ān says:

> God is He who has created the heavens and the earth, and all that is between them, in six days; and sits upon the Throne. (al-Sajdah 32: 4)

> And it is He who is God in heaven and God on earth; He is the All-wise, the All-knowing. Glory be to Him, to whom belongs the kingdom of the heavens and the earth and all that is between them. (Zukhruf 43: 84–5)

> Why, had there been gods in earth and heaven other than God, both would surely have gone to ruin. (al-Anbiyā' 21: 22)

> That God is then your Lord, the Creator of everything; there is no god but He. How then are you perverted? (al-Mu'min 40: 62)

> That God is then your Lord; to Him belongs the sovereignty; there is no god but He. How then are you turned about? (al-Zumar 39: 6)

> He is God; there is no god but He. He is the Sovereign King, the All-holy, the Source of peace, the Keeper of faith, the All-preserver, the All-mighty, the All-compeller, the One to whom all greatness belongs. (al-Ḥashr 59: 23)

> Surely God does not wrong so much as an atom's weight. (al-Nisā' 4: 40)

> Perfect are the words of your Lord in truthfulness and justice. (al-An'ām 6: 115)

6 The Qur'ān says:

> And I have not created Jinn and mankind except to serve Me. (al-Dhāriyāt 51: 56)

> Judgement (as to what is right and what is wrong) belongs only to God; He has commanded that you shall not serve any but Him. That is the right way; but most men know not. (Yūsuf 12: 40)

> And say not, as to what your tongues falsely describe: this is lawful, and this is unlawful, thus forging lies against God; surely those who forge lies against God shall not prosper. (al-Naḥl 16: 116)

7 The Qur'ān says:

There shall certainly come to you guidance from Me, then he who follows My guidance shall not go astray, neither shall he be unhappy. (Ṭā Hā 20: 123)

All mankind was one community; [when they began to differ] then God raised up the prophets as heralds of good tidings and as warners; and He sent down with them the Book with the Truth, that He might decide between people regarding what they differed in. (al-Baqarah 2: 213)

Indeed, We have sent forth among every people a Messenger, (saying): Serve God only, and shun all powers in rebellion against God. (al-Naḥl 16: 36)

We have not ever sent any Messenger but that he should be obeyed, by God's leave. (al-Nisā' 4: 64)

8 The Qur'ān says:

Surely We shall call to account those unto whom a message was sent, and surely We shall call to account the message-bearers. (al-'Arāf 7: 6)

Blessed be He in whose hand is the kingdom, He has power over everything, He who has created death and life, that He might test which of you is best in conduct. (al-Mulk 67: 1–2)

Unto God shall you return, all of you, then He will tell you what you had been doing. (al-Mā'idah 5: 105)

And you will surely be called to account for all that you ever did. (al-Naḥl 16: 93)

When the book [of deeds] shall be laid open, then you will see the guilty fearful at what is in it, and saying: Alas for us! What a book is this! It leaves out nothing, small or great, but it has taken into account. (al-Kahf 18: 49)

And so, he who has done an atom's weight of good, shall see it; and he who has done an atom's weight of evil shall see it. (al-Zalzalah 99: 7–8)

And, hide your thoughts or state them openly, He knows all that is in hearts. (al-Mulk 67: 13)

9 The Qur'ān says:

> And there are some men who sell their selves, seeking God's pleasure; and God is most compassionate towards His servants. O Believers, surrender yourselves wholly unto God. (al-Baqarah 2: 207–8)

> Now there has come to you from God Light, and a clear Book, through which God guides those who follow His pleasure, to the paths of peace, and brings them out of the depths of darkness into the light, by His leave; and He guides them onto a straight path. (al-Mā'idah 5: 15–16)

10 The Qur'ān says:

> Verily you are the best people raised unto mankind, you enjoin good and forbid evil and you are believers in God. (Āl 'Imrān 3: 110)

> If We establish them [the Muslims] in the land (give them power), they establish Prayers, give Alms, enjoin good and forbid evil – with God rests the end [decisions] of all affairs. (al-Ḥajj 22: 41)

Chapter 3

1 For a detailed exposition, see Mawdudi, *Islamic Law and Constitution*, Lahore 1960, Ch. 4.

2 The Qur'ān says:

> Then, Exalted be God, the Sovereign King, the True. There is no god but He, the Lord of the Noble Throne. (al-Mu'minūn 23: 116)

> To Him belongs the sovereignty over the heavens and the earth; He gives life, and He makes to die, and He has power over everything. (al-Ḥadīd 57: 2)

> Say: Who is it that provides you out of heaven and earth, or who is it that has full power over hearing and sight, and who is it that brings forth the living out of the dead, and brings forth the dead out of the living? And who is it that governs in all matters? They will surely say: God. (Yūnus 10: 31)

63

Verily, to Him belongs all creation and all authority. Blessed be God, the Lord of all the worlds. (al-A'rāf 7: 54)

Also see notes 5 and 6 on p. 61.

3 The Qur'ān says:

Follow what has been sent down to you from your Lord, and follow no masters other than Him; little do you remember. (al-A'rāf 7: 3)

Say: Have you considered that, of what God has sent down for you as sustenance, you have made some unlawful, and some lawful? Say: Has God given you leave [to do this], or do you forge lies against God? (Yūnus 10: 59)

Whoso judges not according to what God has sent down – they are the disbelievers . . . they are the wrongdoers . . . they are the transgressors. (al-Mā'idah 5: 44–7)

It is not for any believing man or believing woman, when God and His Messenger have decided a matter, to have any choice for themselves in their affairs. For whoever rebels against God and His Messenger has gone astray into manifest error. (al-Aḥzāb 33: 36)

4 The Qur'ān says:

And We have sent you unto all mankind a Messenger; God suffices for a witness. Whoever obeys the Messenger, he has indeed obeyed God; and (if) one turns away, We have not sent you to be a keeper. (al-Nisā' 4: 79–80)

Say: If you love God, follow me; God will love you, and forgive you your sins. (Āl 'Imrān 3: 31)

[The Prophet] who enjoins upon them the doing of right and forbids them the doing of wrong, and makes lawful for them the good things and makes unlawful for them the bad things, and lifts from them their burdens, and the shackles that were upon them . . . Say: O Mankind, I am the Messenger of God to you all, of Him to whom belongs the sovereignty over the heavens and the earth. There is no god but He. He gives life and He makes to die. (al-A'rāf 7: 157–8)

Verily, in the Messenger of God there is a good example for you, for him who has hopes in God and the last day, and remembers God often. (al-Aḥzāb 33: 21)

Whatever the Messenger gives you, take; whatever he forbids you, give over; and fear God. (al-Ḥashr 59: 7)

But, by your Lord, they do not believe unless they make you the judge in whatever matters arise between them, and then they find not in their hearts any impediment regarding what you have decided; but surrender in full submission. (al-Nisā' 4: 65)

Also see note 7 on p. 62.

5 The Qur'ān says:

And, remember, when your Lord said to the angels: I am going to establish upon earth a vicegerent. (al-Baqarah 2: 30)

O David, We have made you a vicegerent on earth; judge, then, between men with justice, and follow not vain desire, lest it lead you astray from the way of God. (Ṣād 38: 26)

It is He who has made you vicegerents on the earth, and has raised some of you in ranks above others, so that He may test you in what He has given you. (al-An'ām 6: 165)

6 This promise is for *all* Muslims:

God has promised all those of you who believe and do good works that He will surely make them gain power on earth, even as He made those gain power who were before them. (al-Nūr 24: 55)

The Qur'ān further says:

Their affairs are [decided] by consultation between themselves. (al-Shūrā 42: 38)

And take counsel with them in all matters. (Āl 'Imrān 3: 159)

There are many Hadith too. In one Hadith, 'Alī says:

I asked Allah's Messenger, blessings and peace be on him, we may face matters, after you, about which nothing in the Qur'ān has come down nor has anything been heard from you? The Prophet, blessings and peace be on him, said:

Collect the believing servants from my Ummah and decide it by consultation among yourselves, and decide not by the opinion of any one individual. (Ālūsī, *Rūḥ al-Ma'ānī*)

In another, 'Umar says:

If anyone invites to his own rule or that of someone else, without consultation between Muslims, then you will fail in your duty if you do not kill him. (*Kanz al-'Ummāl*, Vol. 5)

Ibn 'Abbās also narrates:

God and His Messenger do not need any consultation; only that God has prescribed it as mercy for my Ummah. He who decides by consultation will find the right way, but he who gives up consultation will not find the right way. (*Baihaqī*)

7 For a detailed study of all these and other relevant points as presented by the author, see *Islamic Law and Constitution*, op. cit., Ch. 4, Sec. IV and V; Ch. 5, Sec. III, V and VI; Ch. 6, Sec. IV.

8 The Qur'ān says:

Who, if We grant them power on earth, they establish the Prayer, and give Alms, and enjoin the doing of right and forbid the doing of wrong. (al-Ḥajj 22: 41)

Indeed, We sent Our Messengers with clear signs, and We sent down with them the Book and the Balance, so that men might uphold justice. (al-Ḥadīd 57: 25)

Surely God enjoins justice, and the doing of good and giving to kinsfolk, and He forbids all indecency, bad deeds, and transgressions. (al-Naḥl 16: 90)

9 The Qur'ān, in many places, instructs Muslims to abide by moral laws in all affairs of state:

And never let hatred of anyone lead you to not doing justice, be just – that is nearer to God-fearing. (al-Ma'idah 5: 8)

And be not like [a woman] who breaks her yarn, after she has spun it and made strong, into fibres, by taking your oaths as a [means of] deception among yourselves, so that one people may become more powerful than others. God only tests you thereby; and certainly He will make clear to you on the Day of Resurrection all that on which you used to differ. (al-Naḥl 16: 92)

And never let your hatred of the people who bar you from the Holy Mosque lead you to transgression. Help one another in good and righteousness, and do not help one another in evil and enmity. (al-Ma'idah 5: 2)

And fight in the way of God those who fight you, but transgress not: God loves not transgressors . . . Whoso transgresses against you, you transgress against him like he has transgressed against you; and fear God, and remember that God is with the God-fearing. (al-Baqarah 2: 190–4)

(Except) those of the idolators with whom you made covenant, if they have not failed you and neither have lent support to anyone against you, fulfil your covenant with them till their term; surely God loves the God-fearing. (al-Tawbah 9: 4)

And if you fear treachery from people [with whom you have made a covenant], renounce it in an equitable manner; surely God loves not the treacherous. (al-Anfāl 8: 58)

10 For a comprehensive discussion on this point, see the author's *Fundamental Rights of Man*, Lahore, 1960. Also, *Islamic Law and Constitution*, op. cit., Ch. 6, Sec. VII and Ch. 7, Sec. IX and X.

11 Some of the points referred to here can materialise only when the Islamic state has attained its final form. As far as the transitory phase is concerned efforts should be made to approach them as nearly as possible.

12 There are many Hadith which establish that Islam is the ruling condition for eligibility to citizenship in a truly Islamic state:

Anyone who testifies that there is no god but God, and turns towards our Qibla, and observes our Prayer, and eats of our slaughtered animals, he then is the Muslim, to whom are due all the rights of a Muslim and on whom are all the obligations of a Muslim. (*Bukhārī*)

O mankind, listen, your Lord is One; there is no superiority for an Arab over a non-Arab, nor for a non-Arab over an Arab, nor for a black over a red, nor for a red over a black – except on the basis of God-consciousness. (*Baihaqī, Rūḥ al-Ma'ānī*)

Listen and obey, even if a negro slave is made your ruler. (*Bukhārī*)

67

13 For details, see *Islamic Law and Constitution*, op. cit., Ch. 8.

14 See ibid., Ch. 6, Sec. IV, V and VI.

Chapter 4

1 Those who are interested in pursuing this subject are referred to *Purdah and the Status of Women in Islam*, Lahore, 1972, *Ḥuqūq al-Zawjayn* (Urdu), Lahore, 1919, and *Studies in the Family Laws of Islam*, ed. Khurshid Ahmad, Karachi, 1961.

2 The Qur'ān says:

> O mankind, We have created you all of a male and a female, and have made you races and tribes, that you may recognise one another. Surely the noblest of you in the sight of God is the most God-conscious of you. God is All-knowing, All-aware. (al-Ḥujurāt 49: 13)

Allah's Messenger, blessings and peace be on him, said:

> I bear witness [said the Prophet], that all mankind is one brotherhood. (*Abū Dā'ūd*)

> All creation is the family of God; of them God loves him more who does more good to His family. (*Mishkāwt*)

3 Allah's Messenger, blessings and peace be on him, declared this principle clearly and unequivocally:

> There is no higher status for an Arab over a non-Arab, nor for a non-Arab over an Arab: you are all children of Adam; and Adam was created from dust. (*Bukhārī* and *Muslim*)

The Qur'ān says:

> All Believers indeed are brothers. (al-Ḥujurāt 49: 10)

> Surely this community of yours is one single community, and I am your Lord; so serve Me. (al-Anbiyā' 21: 92)

> Yet if they repent, and establish Prayer, and pay Alms, then they become your brothers in faith. (al-Tawbah 9: 11)

Those who have believed, and migrated, and struggled with their possessions and their selves in the way of God, as well as those who have given shelter and help – those are the friends of one another. (al-Anfāl 8: 72)

4 The Qur'ān says:

O mankind, fear your Lord, who has created you of a single soul, and from it has created its mate, and from the pair of them spread abroad many men and women. And fear God in whose name you demand from one another, and of these ties of kinship. (al-Nisā' 4: 1)

5 Some Qur'ānic injunctions, moral and legal, in this regard are:

And come not near adultery; surely it is an abomination, and an evil way. (al-Isrā' 17: 32)

The adulteress and the adulterer – flog each of them with a hundred stripes, and let not compassion with them seize you in the matter of the law of God. (al-Nūr 24: 2)

6 The Qur'ān clearly forbids permissiveness in society:

Those who love that indecency should be spread among the Believers – there awaits them a painful chastisement in the present world and the world to come. (al-Nūr 24: 19)

For teachings regarding inter-mixing between sexes, see: al-Nūr 24: 27–9, 30–1, 58–61; al-Aḥzāb 33: 32–3, 53–5, 59.

7 The Qur'ān also says:

. . . Also [forbidden to you are] all married women other than those you rightfully possess [through wedlock]: this is God's ordinance, binding upon you. Lawful for you, beyond all these, are all you may seek, offering them of your possessions, taking them in honest wedlock, and not in license . . . (al-Nisā' 4: 24)

And marry the single from among you as well as such of your male and female slaves as are fit for marriage. If they are poor [let this not deter you] God will grant them sufficiency out of His bounty. (al-Nūr 24: 32–3)

Allah's Messenger, blessings and peace be on him, said:

Young men, whosoever can marry, should marry. (*Bukhārī* and *Muslim*)

Whoever marries, he completes one-half of religion. (*Mishkāwt*)

8 The Qur'ān mentions this principle thus:

Men are responsible for women, because of what God has bestowed more on some of them than the other, and for what they may spend of their possessions. (al-Nisā' 4: 34)

9 The Qur'ān, in this regard, says:

It is He who has created you out of a single soul, and a mate of like nature, as its spouse; that he might live with her (in love and comfort). (al-A'rāf 7: 189)

And among His wonders is that He creates for you, of your own kind, spouses that you live with them, and He has set between you love and mercy. Surely in that are signs for the people who think. (al-Rūm 30: 21)

They [women] are as a garment for you [men], and you [men] as a garment for them [women]. (al-Baqarah 2: 187)

To men the share from what they earn, and to women the share from what they earn. (al-Nisā' 4: 32)

And when you divorce women . . . then retain them in a fair manner or let them go in a fair manner. But do not detain them by force [against their will] in order to harm [them] and to transgress; whoever does so wrongs indeed himself. Take not God's command in a frivolous spirit . . . and when you divorce women . . . hinder them not from marrying other men if they have agreed with each other in a fair manner. (al-Baqarah 2: 231–2)

10 The Qur'ān says:

And when We took pledge from the children of Israel: You shall serve none but God, and be good to your parents, and the near of kin, and the orphans, and the poor; and speak to people in a good way. (al-Baqarah 2: 83)

They question you regarding what they should spend. Say: whatever of your wealth you spend shall [first] be for your parents, and for the near of kin . . . (al-Baqarah 2: 215)

11 Allah's Messenger, blessings and peace be on him, said:

Tie of blood-relation (*rahm*) is derived from *al-Rahmān* (the Most-merciful), and God says to it: Whoever keeps you, I shall join him; and whoever severs you, I shall sever connection with him. (*Bukhārī*)

One who severs ties of blood-relation shall not enter Paradise. (*Bukhārī* and *Muslim*)

See *Mishkāwt*, chapter on 'Kindness and Joining Ties of Blood-Relation'.

12 The Qur'ān says:

And do good to parents, and near kinsmen, and to orphans, and to the needy, and to the neighbour who is of kin, and to the neighbour who is a stranger, and to the companion at your side. (al-Nisā' 4: 36)

13 It is part of an elaborate Hadith narrated by Ṭabarānī:

One of the Companions of the Prophet, blessings and peace be on him, enquired: O Messenger of Allah, what is the duty of a neighbour towards his neighbours? He replied: If he asks for a loan, you should give him a loan; if he wants your help, you should help him; if he be sick, you should go to see him; if he be needy you should try to fulfil his need; if he gets good news, you should congratulate him; if any calamity befalls him, it is your duty to console him; if he dies, you should attend his funeral; you should not raise your walls to such a height that they obstruct the ventilation of your neighbour's house, even he be willing; do not tantilise your neighbour with the smell of your delicious food unless you send a portion of it to him; if you bring fruit into your house then send some to your neighbour; otherwise keep it hidden from your neighbour, and you should also be careful that your children do not take some out, else the children of your neighbour may feel disappointed.

71

Chapter 5

1 Those who want to study further the author's exposition of the Islamic economic system are referred to the following: 'Economic and Political Teachings of the Qur'ān' in *A History of Muslim Philosophy*, ed. M. M. Sharif, Wiesbaden, 1963, Vol. I, pp. 178–90; *Islam awr Jadīd Ma'āshī Naẓariyāt* (Islam and Modern Economic Ideologies – Urdu), Lahore; *Sūd*, (Interest – Urdu), 2 vols., Lahore, 1948–1952; *Islam awr 'Adl-i-Ijtimā'ī* (Islam and Social Justice – Urdu), Lahore, 1963.

2 The Qur'ān says:

> O Mankind, serve your Lord who has created you, and those before you, so that you might be God-fearing, who has made the earth a resting place for you and the sky an edifice, and has sent down out of the sky water, and thereby has brought forth fruits as your provision. (al-Baqarah 2: 21–2)

> It is He who has created for you all that is on earth. (al-Baqarah 2: 29)

> Indeed We have established you on earth and provided thereon means of livelihood for you. (al-A'rāf 7: 10)

> It is God who has created the heavens and the earth, and who sends down water from the sky, and thereby brings forth fruits as your provision. And He has made subservient to you ships so that they may sail through the seas at His behest; and He has made subservient to you the rivers, and He has made subservient to you the sun and moon, constant upon their courses, and He has made subservient to you the night and day. And He gives you of all you ask Him. (Ibrāhīm 14: 32–4)

> Some Hadith describe the value of wealth for a Believer:

> Anyone who acquires it lawfully and spends it lawfully, for him it is the best helper. (*Muslim*)

> What a good helper is wealth in maintaining God-consciousness. (*Kanz al-'Ummāl*)

3 Allah's Messenger, blessings and peace be on him, declared thus:

> All human beings have a share in water, pasture and fire. (*Abū 'Ubayd, Kitāb al-Amwāl*)

All Muslims have a share in three things: water, pasture and fire. (*Abū Dā'ūd*)

4 Abū Yūsuf (peace be on him) relates a Hadith, on the authority of Ṭawūs, in his *Kitāb al-Kharāj*:

The deserted plot of land (having no owner) belongs to God, His Prophet and then to yourself. A deserted plot of land will be the property of the one who brings it into use and anyone who does not make use of it for three consecutive years will have no right to it after the expiry of the said period.

Again it has been narrated by Abū Yūsuf, on the authority of Sālim Ibn 'Abdullah Zahrī, that once 'Umar during his reign declared from the pulpit of the mosque:

A deserted plot of land will be the property of anyone who brings it in use and anyone who does not make use of it for three years will have no right to it whatsoever.

5 Discussing the law derived from the above-mentioned Hadith, Abū Yūsuf states:

According to our view (i.e. the Ḥanafī view) the land was not previously owned by anyone and if the same is brought in use by someone, he has a rightful proprietary claim over it.

6 The Qur'ān says:

Men shall have a share in what parents and kinsfolk leave behind, and women shall have a share in what parents and kinsfolk leave behind, whether it be little or much – the share ordained [by God]. (al-Nisā' 4: 7)

O Believers, spend of the good things you have earned, and of that We have brought forth for you from the earth. (al-Baqarah 2: 267)

7 The Qur'ān alludes to this variety as below:

We have distributed between them their means of livelihood in the life of this world and raised some of them above others in rank, so that they might avail themselves of one another's help. (Zukhruf 43: 32)

And on some of you God has bestowed more abundant means of sustenance than on others. (al-Naḥl 16: 71)

73

Do not covet the bounties which God has bestowed more abundantly on some of you than others. Men shall have a share from what they earn, and women shall have a share from what they earn. (al-Nisā' 4: 32)

8 The Qur'ān focuses on social justice as below:

Take him, and shackle him, and then roast him in Hell, then with a chain of seventy cubits' length tie him! He believed not in God, and he urged not the feeding of the needy. (al-Ḥāqqah 69: 30–4)

And they ask you what should they spend; say: Whatever you can spare. (al-Baqarah 2: 219)

Seek, by means of what God has granted you, the life to come, and forget not your share of the present world; and do good as God has done good to you; and seek not to spread corruption on earth. (al-Qaṣaṣ 28: 77)

Similarly, Allah's Messenger, blessings and peace be on him, and his Companions, once they had the political power, were fully cognisant of the need and importance of social justice and the duty of the Islamic state in this regard:

God and His Messenger [says the Prophet] are responsible for one who has no one to care for him. (*Tirmidhī*)

Even if a camel dies unattended [says 'Umar] on the bank of the river Euphrates, I fear that God will take me to task for that. (*Ibn S'ad*)

9 The Qur'ān says:

O Believers, eat not of one another's wealth wrongfully, except that there be trading by your agreeing together. (al-Nisā' 4: 29)

And eat not of one another's wealth wrongfully, and neither employ legal artifices with a view to eating sinfully, and knowingly, anything that by right belongs to others. (al-Baqarah 2: 188)

Give, therefore, full measure and weight [in all your dealings] and do not deprive people of what is rightfully theirs; and do not spread corruption on earth, after it has been set right. (al-A'rāf 7: 85)

10 The Qur'ān says:

O Believers, do not make unlawful the good things which God has made lawful for you, and transgress not; surely God does not love the transgressors. And, partake of the lawful good things which God has provided you and fear God in whom you believe. (al-Mā'idah 5: 87)

And eat and drink but do not waste; verily He does not love the wasteful. (al-A'rāf 7: 31)

And give his due to the near of kin, as well as to the needy and the wayfarer, but do not squander [your wealth] senselessly, the squanderers are indeed the brothers of the Satans. (al-Isrā' 17: 26–7)

They who, whenever they spend, are neither wasteful nor niggardly; it is always a just mean between these two. (al-Furqān 25: 67)

11 See al-Nisā' 4: 7–13.

Chapter 6

1 The Qur'ān explains man's free-will and responsibility for his actions:

We did offer the trust [of reason and volition] to heaven and earth and the mountains, but they refused to bear it, and they were afraid of it; but man bore it, surely he is [capable of being] great wrongdoer, very foolish – so that God may punish the hypocrites, men and women, and the idolators, men and women; and that God may turn in His mercy unto the believing men and believing women; and God is All-forgiving, All-merciful. (al-Aḥzāb 33: 72–3)

2 The Qur'ān states clearly that God does not desire asceticism:

And monastic asceticism they [Christians] invented, We did not enjoin it upon them; but only the seeking of the pleasure of God [did We enjoin]; but they observed it not as it ought to have been observed. (al-Ḥadīd 57: 27)

Allah's Messenger, blessings and peace be on him, also took special care to bring this point home. One Hadith says:

75

Abū Umāmah, Allah be pleased with him, says: Once we went on an expedition with Allah's Messenger, blessings and peace be on him, when a man passed by a cave which had water and greenery. He said to himself that he would renounce this world and stay in this cave, for which he asked permission from the Prophet. The Prophet said: I have not been raised with Judaism or Christianity, but I have been raised with a religion which requires turning away from everything to God and which is easy. By the One in whose hand is Muhammad's life, a morning or evening spent struggling in the way of Allah is better than this world and whatever it contains; and standing in a row to fight is better than praying for sixty years. (*Aḥmad*)

3 The Qur'ān says:

O Believers, attain to true faith in God and His Messenger and the Book He has sent down on His Messenger. (al-Nisā' 4: 136)

Surely God's friends – no fear shall be on them, neither shall they sorrow – are those who have attained to true faith, and are God-fearing. (Yūnus 10: 63)

4 The Qur'ān says:

Say: God's guidance is the true guidance, and we are commanded to surrender to the Lord of all worlds. (al-An'ām 6: 71)

When his Lord said to him [Abraham]: Surrender, he readily said: I have surrendered to the Lord of all worlds. (al-Baqarah 2: 131)

Whoever obeys God and the Messenger, they are among those whom God has blessed: among the prophets, and the truthful, and the martyrs, and the righteous. Good companions they are! (al-Nisā' 4: 69)

Whoso obeys God and His Messenger, and fears God and is conscious of Him – it is they who shall triumph. (al-Nūr 24: 52)

5 The Qur'ān defines *taqwā* very comprehensively:

It is not piety that you turn your faces towards the east or the west; but true piety (is of his) who believes in God, and the

Last Day, and the angels, and the Book, and the prophets; and gives away his wealth, however cherished, to kinsmen, and orphans, and the needy, and the wayfarer, and the beggars, and for the freeing of human beings from bondage; and who performs Prayer, and pays the Zakāt; and they who fulfil their promises whenever they promise, and endure with fortitude misfortune, hardship and peril: it is they who are true in their faith and it is they who are *Muttaqīn* (God-conscious). (al-Baqarah 2: 177)

6 In a long Hadith narrated by 'Umar, Allah's Messenger, blessings and peace be on him, while answering a number of questions asked by Gabriel, defined *Iḥsān* thus:

That you serve God as if you are seeing Him; if you do not see Him, He is seeing you. (*Muslim*)

The Qur'ān defines *iḥsān* in terms of striving and struggling in His cause:

Many a prophet there has been, with whom many God-devoted men have fought, and they fainted not for what they had to suffer in God's way, neither weakened, nor did they abase themselves; and God loves the patient. Nothing else they said but: Lord, forgive us our sins, and that we exceeded in our doings, and make firm our steps, and help us against the people who are disbelievers. And God granted them the rewards of this world and the fairest rewards of the world to come; and God loves the godly. (Āl 'Imrān 3: 146–8)

7 For a more detailed discussion of *īmān, islām, taqwā* and *iḥsān*, see the author's *The Islamic Movement: Dynamics of Values, Power and Change,* Islamic Foundation, Leicester, 1984.

8 The Qur'ān says:

Verily I am God; there is no god but I; therefore serve Me; and establish the Prayer to remember Me. (Ṭā Hā 20: 14)

And establish the Prayer; for Prayer restrains [man] from indecency and all bad deeds; and remembrance of God is great. (al-'Ankabūt 29: 45)

Proclaim your Lord's limitless glory and praise Him before the rising of the sun and before its setting, and extol His glory during some of the hours of the night, and at the ends of the day. (Ṭā Hā 20: 130)

77

And bow down in Prayer with all who thus bow down. (al-Baqarah 2: 43)

9 The Qur'ān describes the purpose of Fasting:

O Believers, Fasting is ordained for you as it was ordained for those before you, so that you may become God-conscious. (al-Baqarah 2: 183)

10 The Qur'ān clearly states that the objective of spending wealth should be only to please God; and that it is a means of human purification and growth:

Take Alms of their wealth, so that you may cleanse them thereby and make them grow in purity. (al-Tawbah 9: 103)

What you give in Alms, seeking God's countenance – it is they who shall have their recompense multiplied. (al-Rūm 30: 39)

And from it [the Fire] shall keep away the most God-conscious, he who gives his wealth to purify himself, conferring no favour on anyone to be repaid, only seeking the countenance of his Lord, the Most High, and soon he shall surely be well-pleased. (al-Layl 92: 17–21)

11 This paragraph has been added from the author's work *Towards Understanding Islam*, Islamic Foundation, Leicester, 1981.

That Jihad is the measure of the truthfulness of claim to faith and stands highest in order of priority among all good acts has been clearly stated:

The [true] Believers are those who have attained to faith in God and His Messenger, then have not doubted; and who strive hard with their possessions and their selves in the way of God; it is they who are the truthful ones. (al-Ḥujurāt 49: 15)

Have you made the giving of water to the pilgrims and the inhabiting of the Holy Mosque the same as [the work of] one who believes in God and the Last Day and strives hard in the way of God? Not equal are they in God's eyes. And God guides not people who do wrong. Those who believe, and who have forsaken their homes, and have striven hard in the way of God with their possessions and their selves, attain the highest rank in the sight of God; and it is they who shall triumph! (al-Tawbah 9: 19–22)